COL. JAMES LACKEY

SILVER WINGS

A STEP BY STEP GUIDE TO GO FROM PEDESTRIAN TO AIR FORCE PILOT

This book is the sum total of all my years in the Air Force, especially my experience in Air Education and Training Command. 100% of the profits of this book go to the Air Warrior Courage Foundation, formed by military aviators to "care for our own." This foundation provides financial assistance for medical, educational, and other extraordinary expenses, not covered by others. More information on this amazing organization can be found at:

www.airwarriorcourage.com

CONTENTS

THANK YOU

Writing this book would not have been possible without the help of a number of wonderful and amazing people that selflessly gave their time and talent to make my very rough ideas into something readable. Having said this, several people need special recognition.

My incredible wife Katja, who allowed me to take six very long months of temporary duty at Vance Air Force Base making all this possible. She did not volunteer to join the Air Force but she sacrifices and toils in the hardest job there is--a pilot's wife.

To my kids Graeleigh and William, who have grown into inspiring and amazing adults despite their dad being gone more than any parent should while their kids are growing up. They are a true inspiration and very much a reflection of their mother! All that I hope is to leave the world a better place--for them.

A trio of fantastic ladies, Janelle McAlear, Terri Schaefer, and Stephanie Ritter, who made my poor "pilot speak" into coherent, English words. "Additionally, an extra special thank you goes out to Terri Schaefer for introducing me into the mysterious and fascinating world of publishing. Terri literally did the work of four people and made this book happen." Thank you all very much for the countless hours you spent editing my drafts, chasing down obscure information and pictures. You all are the very best friends and truly made this possible.

Captain Courtney Vidt--the very embodiment of an Air Force pilot. Thank you very much for all your help and assistance while I was at Vance

AFB and more importantly for reminding me how the brother/sisterhood of pilots is alive and well. I sleep well knowing professionals like Courtney are guarding the gates!

To Lt Col (Ret) Bill "Shortfinger" Schwertfeger, the man who is the very ideal of courage and sacrifice, he is a true American hero. Shortfinger's time in the hell of the Hanoi Hilton revealed his true character and stands as a shining example to every Air Force pilot. He spends untold hours sponsoring UPT classes at Vance AFB and inspired me to write this book and donate 100% of the profits to the future of USAF aviation.

Major Megan Brandt--thank to you and your team of superstars at Aerospace Physiology who allowed me to sit in your training classes and use all the super-cool training equipment. Your review and editing skills on the Physiology portion of this book were invaluable.

To Colonel Clark Quinn, my Wing Commander while at Vance AFB--none of this would have happened without his foresight and vision by inviting an Air Force Reservist fill in as the Vice Wing Commander. Thank you for not firing me and for listening (nicely) to my C-5 stories.

To Major General John Flournoy and Colonel Karl Goerke--thank you very much for allowing me to step out of my normal role and support the active duty in such a real and meaningful way. Karl's job as the Wing Commander at Scott AFB became infinitely more difficult because I was at Vance. I owe him more than I can express or repay--I will do my best to do just that.

To my Vance family--Chief Speen, Col and Mrs. Cinnamon, Col LaHaye and Col Benford, thank you very much for all your help and making me feel a part of the team. You were always there to support me and you are all great friends. In the end, I got more from you than I gave--you are the very best.

To my Air Force sisters Col Jenkins and Col Mattox--words cannot express how much your support and sympathetic ears meant during some long hard days. You are a constant reminder of the very best that America has to offer and are my true friends forever.

There are a few more people who were involved in the production of this book. Lt Col Rick Karn, Major Brandon Gorab, Major 4K, Lt Kaitlyn O'Brien and Capt Allen Oberlin. Thanks for your input and insight. I am sure I have forgotten someone. Please know this was not intentional as I am so appreciative of the support of so very many people. Thank you all from the bottom of my heart.

And now, for the disclaimer--the views in these book represent those of the author and not the U.S. Air Force.

FORWARD

by Lt Col (Ret) Bill "Shortfinger" Schwertfeger

When asked to write this forward I thought about the best way to approach it and decided to talk to you the same way I talk to the new 71 FTW student pilots, or as I kindly refer to them, my "pups". You see I call them pups because they usually are full of energy, velocity, and have a short attention span. These pups are not too different from the pups you welcome into your home, except now you are the pup and are about to enter our house.

I entered Vance in September 1967 and had my mind set to be the very best student pilot I could be. I did not have a book like this to guide me; instead I only had the words that leaders gave me, and the will to be the best. As you read this book, you will find the guidelines to help you make the transition from Pup to Dog and eventually to Top Dog.

The 52 weeks of training you are considering, or even about to enter, will test you at a degree of intensity that will make your college days seem like a cakewalk. This book will take you through all the phases of pilot training. Read it and then re-read it! As pups, you will be constantly tested mentally, physically, and professionally. You will also be asked to multi-task while flying. Speaking about flying, flying is the most important thing that you must do. Always "Fly the Aircraft First" no matter what else is occurring, and then work to solve whatever problem is at hand.

This book is designed for you to utilize throughout all the phase of pilot training, keep it with you and refer to it daily. The basic principles it discusses will carry you through your transition from the T-6 to the T-1 or T-38, as well as to your follow-on aircraft, and throughout your career. You will find that teamwork, officership, physical conditioning and strength, and most importantly dedication to "be the best," will carry you well in today's Air Force. Remember that even though you must compete against your fellow classmates, you must never leave anybody behind. Help the weakest link in dealing with the demanding challenges that you will face. Also, remember that there is a time and place for you to unwind, blow off some steam, and relax. Just do it responsibly. Having your Squadron Commander get you out of jail will get you kicked out of pilot training and end your career faster than a speeding bullet.

If you are still one of the pups deciding if this is the right path for you, after reading this book, ask yourself, do I have what it will take to be a member of the world's greatest Air Force? Please do not make this decision lightly, for many are vying for a few slots. The thing I do not want to see is you taking one of these precious slots and then quitting early in the program. That slot will be lost forever. I hope that "yes" will be your answer to the question posed above and if so, now the hard work begins! I wish you the best and that sometime in the future you can give back to those pups that will follow in your footsteps.

Lastly, I will leave you, my pups, with some words of wisdom from an Author Unknown.

An ode to those who fly:

"Once the wings go on, they never come off whether they can be seen or not. It fuses to the soul through adversity, fear and adrenaline, and no one who has ever worn them with pride, integrity and guts can ever sleep through the 'call of the wild' that wafts through bedroom windows in the deep of the night. When a good flyer leaves the 'job' and retires, many are jealous, some are pleased and yet others, who may have already retired, wonder. We wonder if he knows what he is leaving behind, because we already know. We know, for example, that after a lifetime of camaraderie that few experience, it will remain as a longing for those past times. We know in the world of flying, there is a fellowship, which lasts long after the flight suits are hung up in the back of the closet. We know even if he throws them away, they will be on him with every step and breath that remains in his life. We also know how the very bearing of the man speaks of what he was and in his heart still is.

Because we flew, we envy no man on earth."

~Author Unknown

Bill "Shortfinger" Schwertfeger

Lt Col, USAF Ret, POW

TOP DOG

INTRODUCTION

This all begins with a very simple question that only you can answer--do you want this life?

Being a pilot in the United States Air Force is one of the greatest adventures left in the world. You literally wake up every day and your job is to fly multi-million dollar aircraft that can operate at the very edge of human endurance, travel thousands of miles, and put weapons on our nation's enemies to protect the homeland. Honestly, that kind of power and excitement is dizzying and humbling at the same time.

Do you want this life?

United States Air Force Specialized Undergraduate Pilot Training (SUPT) is the most difficult training in the U.S. military, period. You may hear some noise about Navy SEALs or Special Operations training being intense, but day in and day out, nothing compares to the mental and physical grind needed to perfect performance in UPT. Every single day your performance is measured and graded. Everything you do has a standard by which you are measured against. Time and again you are pushed to the very limits of stress and anxiety, all designed to extract the very best performance from you. Fail or regress in any arena, whether it be flying, academic, mental, or physical, and you are gone.

Do you want this life?

Best of all, Air Force flight school is the last true meritocracy left in the modern world. Your success here does not rely on your gender, wealth, family name, connections, college, or degree. Once you get to pilot training, only your performance determines your outcome. Read that again and let it sink in. Where else in life does your performance solely determine your outcome? Fly well, study hard, and perform under pressure and you win. If you freeze under pressure, let self-doubt creep into your brain, or just plain choke, you will be doing something else for a living.

So, why is flight school so hard? Because it is worth it! Flight school is hard because at its heart, you are being trained to use an aircraft as a weapon of war. Combat aviation is the ultimate test of the air warrior and is brutally unforgiving in its application. The beauty of United States Air Force flight training is that once you earn your wings, you will not only have the skills to safely fly, but also the ability to adapt and overcome anything life can throw at you. An old saying we had when I was an instructor pilot was, "I can teach a monkey how to fly but I can't teach him to think when everything goes to shit." Air Force pilots have to think and overcome adversity on a daily basis. By earning your wings, you show the world and yourself that you have surpassed the most demanding military training in the world. That kind of victory leaves a mark on your soul-- forever.

But you have to ask yourself -- do you want this life?

Think you have what it takes to earn those silver wings? The Air Force won't give them to you, but if you have what it takes, make the commitment to earn them, and work a little every day to realize your dream, you *will* earn a pair for yourself.

So who is this book written for? My ideal readers are:

1. • Any young American between 17 and 20 years of age, currently in high school or college and searching for the ultimate challenge.

2. • The person who has graduated from college and entered a career that is just not fulfilling. A lifetime of long commutes in order to sit under florescent lights in a cube farm is sucking your will to live.

3. • An enlisted person from the Air Force, Army, Navy, Marines, or Coast Guard who has seen what military aviation looks like and would like to join the pilot ranks.

The perfect subject has always thought about being a pilot and loves to challenge him or herself with being part of the very best in all areas of their lives. A solid student, competent athlete, and enough of a homebody geek to stay out of legal trouble will have no trouble going through the wickets to get accepted into the program. You do *not* have to be a math genius, captain of the football team, or a monk to be a fantastic pilot. The well-rounded person makes the best pilot candidate.

Although, I am describing the ideal, do not let this description discourage you! It is never too late to make a radical change in your life and pursue your dreams--you never know if you can do it unless you try!

This book is a career's worth of advice, all enclosed in a couple hundred pages and condenses what I have seen, stories I have heard, and firsthand views of Undergraduate Pilot Training--basically a catalogue of where other students have failed on the road to earning their pilot wings. I have tried to lay out factual information, good ideas, proven techniques, and realistic strategies to take you from where you are today to pinning a set of silver wings on your chest. My main goal is to strip away the mystery of Undergraduate Pilot Training and show that the pipeline, the training, and the career it unlocks is logical, fair, and attainable to virtually anyone.

Over the years, I have consistently seen two groups of people that excelled at pilot training, not because they were more gifted when they walked in the door to UPT but because they were better prepared than their peers: 1) Offspring of Air Force pilots. (Because they know the lifestyle and know what is important to study) and 2) Students that arrived from particular Air Guard and Reserve units. Their units usually have a very long and involved hiring process and spend a tremendous amount of time prepping their students well before they arrive at training. Think; group one, on steroids. The genesis of this book is to remove the mystery and give you a preview of what to expect. This will put you in the same arena as those other two groups.

Along the way, I'll clue you in to booby traps, pitfalls, and the honest truth of what USAF pilot training is all about.

What this book is *not* is a checklist that will spoon-feed you the program. It does not contain the course syllabus or spell out the training objectives for each sortie you will fly in pilot training. It is an addition for your mental toolbox and will help keep you from being surprised during the most difficult military training program.

DECIDE NOW

Decide now if you want to become an Air Force pilot. Completing pilot training is a fantastic lifetime achievement, a golden moment in your life, and becoming a pilot is a dream come true for many people--myself included. However, before accepting that pilot slot and starting down the path of attending Undergraduate Pilot Training, you have to make the commitment in your own mind and decide if you want those silver wings more than anything else. Too many times I have conducted the final interview with student pilots after they quit pilot training and I have heard the most ridiculous reasons why they quit. Here is just a sample:

- *I didn't realize pilot training would take so much work.*

4

- *My recruiter/ROTC instructor/Academy squadron commander said that I should try the pilot route first and if I don't like it I can always quit.*

- *Undergraduate Pilot Training is not what I thought it would be.*

- *I didn't know that learning to be a pilot takes so many hours per day.*

- *I'm uncomfortable with directly or indirectly killing people.*

Not every person can be an Air Force pilot! The hand-eye coordination needed for safe flying alone is a high bar to achieve. Add in the intelligence and physical requirements and it is easy to see why only one person in 500 will walk across the stage to receive their wings. Having said all of that, though, it is also a requirement for every potential pilot candidate to look into their own soul and answer the question--do I want those silver wings?

If the answer is "Yes," you have to lock it away in your soul and focus your mind, body, and spirit to making it happen. All other things have to take a back seat to your dream. Remember, this is a special achievement. Air Force pilot wings are not meant for everyone. If someone has to pressure you into going to flight school in the first place and drag you across the finish line, then the wings are not really earned, are they?

Once you make the decision to earn your wings and dare to live an extraordinary life, get on with it!

So who am I to give you this information? I have had the honor and privilege to serve in virtually every aspect of the USAF pilot training program. From beginning to end, I have seen the entire Undergraduate Pilot Training program from both the inside and outside, and I have a wealth of experience to pass on.

I entered UPT as a student pilot at Vance AFB, class 90-02 in November 1988. After graduation a year later, I was selected as an instructor pilot in the T-38 Talon and remained at Vance AFB. In a bid to earn a fighter assignment, I took a position as an instructor/contract administrator pilot in the T-41 Mescalero aircraft (Cessna 172) at the Hondo airport in Texas. In this role, I supervised Doss Aviation Corp while they oversaw the Flight

Screening Program, which eventually became the Initial Flight Training program, now located in Pueblo, Colorado.

I went on to fly C-12 and C-5 aircraft in the operational Air Force. After years in the C-5 Galaxy, I had the unique opportunity to go back and serve as the vice wing commander at Vance AFB. In this role, I filled a key leadership position and again taught student pilots the art and science of aviation. Along the way, I have influenced the training of literally hundreds of student pilots and directly instructed in the slowest (T-41), the fastest trainer (T-38), and the largest (C-5) Air Force aircraft.

It was during this time as the vice wing commander that I realized the greatest influence I can have on future Air Force pilot production was to write a book that removes the mystery and misinformation of Specialized Undergraduate Pilot Training. This book seeks to gather a lot of threads of information from different sources and put the important data in front of you--so you can make an informed decision if you want to live an extraordinary life. Besides, the Air Force needs pilots!

A note about style--I have been told that I write the way I talk. I am decidedly un-politically correct and I use cuss words, a lot. This is a truthful undertaking, not a PC, scholarly paper. If this kind of language and style bothers you, please stop reading now. I have strong opinions on the pilot training subject; if you listen to the essence of the information I am imparting, you will do well at Undergraduate Pilot Training, it is just that simple.

Finally, life is all about what you leave behind and the sun is beginning to set on my Air Force career. I know that I have a finite time to serve in the Air Force and I want to pass on a lot of hard earned knowledge. Perhaps I can build a legacy in the process. When all my time is done and I close my eyes for the very last time, I will take comfort knowing that I had a hand in fielding the next generation of pilots that defend America. What more could a man ask for?

Being an Air Force pilot is an incredible life and career--one that is well worth the time and effort. Take my word for it--you want this life!

GET MOTIVATED!

The graveyard is the richest place on Earth, because it is here that you will find all the hopes and dreams that were never fulfilled, the books that were never written, the songs that were never sung, the inventions that were never shared, the cures that were never discovered, all because someone was too afraid to take that first step, keep with the problem, or determined to carry out their dream.

Les Brown

What do you want to do with your life?

Does the idea of zipping along at 500 miles per hour, 100 feet off the ground excite you? How about delivering hundreds of thousands of pounds worth of critically needed supplies to a humanitarian disaster and literally saving lives? Any chance you would be interested in shooting down enemy aircraft? Maybe doling out the ultimate payback of a 30mm gun run on enemy fighters trying to kill our ground troops gets you jazzed.

You can do this--yes you.

Every three weeks, the United States Air Force graduates a class of new pilots from the four training programs at Vance, Columbus, Laughlin, and Sheppard Air Force Bases. Each class numbers around 20+ students and that works out to be over 300 pilots per base, per year. From there, the graduates go on to fly the finest aircraft ever conceived by man. Those new pilots go on to take the most sophisticated jets to the four corners of the world and every place in between. Best of all, no other pilots in the world are more respected than U.S. Air Force pilots. The pilots of the U.S. Air Force are world renowned for being the very best at combat, air refueling, and airlift operations…period.

U.S. Air Force photo/Staff Sgt. Darlene Seltmann

The coolest thing about all this is you can join our ranks. It is a step-by-step process, but if you focus on your goal, devote the time and effort needed to achieve each step, before you know it you will walk across that stage and pin a set of silver wings on your chest. Yes, you can do this!

It takes commitment and work to earn your wings. The Air Force and the world in general will put up plenty of roadblocks along the way to test your resolve and dedication just getting into flight school. The screening process is complex and it can be a gut check of your commitment to achieving your dream.

Once you arrive at your training base, you will enter the crucible of Specialized Undergraduate Pilot Training (SUPT) or just UPT. Air Force pilot training is a rite of passage and the foundation of all Air Force aviation. No matter where you go or what you do in flying, looking at a brother or sister pilot with U. S. Air Force pilot wings on their chest is the ultimate gold standard of quality. At a glance, you know they have gone through the same test of fire that you have and they can complete the mission.

So, how do you actually earn your wings? It is sort of like that old joke about how do you get to Carnegie Hall--practice, practice, practice. How do you earn your pilot wings--commitment, commitment, commitment. Learn the system the Air Force uses to create new pilots, plan your future carefully, and relentlessly execute that plan. If I had to boil it all down to just one word to symbolize what it takes to become an Air Force pilot--tenacity.

Personally, I took the Cortes approach to UPT. When Hernando Cortes came to Mexico in 1519 he faced the entire multi-million strong Aztec Empire with just 600 men, 16 horses, and 11 boats. To inspire his men he uttered three simple words that forever changed the history of the Americas-- "burn the boats." His men set fire to the trans-oceanic ships and destroyed their only line of escape back to Spain. With that phrase, Cortes made it clear to his soldiers; there is no safety or escape behind you--go forward and fight--victory or death! While obviously not that dramatic in my own case, I cleared the decks of my personal life and I had nothing behind me to fall back on, no alternate option in my life or career. I simply had no alternative than to be successful at pilot training. No job prospects, no back-up plans, and no escape clause. All of my family, my girlfriend, and my friends knew I was at flight school and supported me in every way possible. I could not go back without complete failure and abject humiliation. That powerful sword dangling over my head kept me going on some dark days. The reality was clear and simple--succeed in UPT or show to the world that I couldn't cut it. Trust me when I tell you that it worked for me, it kept me motivated, and I studied hard in the moments when I began to doubt myself. More than once I said to myself, "Fuck it, they can throw me out but I am not going to quit." You need to find your own individual motivation. Get on it, now! Just so you know, Cortes' motivation worked, in spades. He defeated the Aztec Empire of over 5 million people and was the first person to conquer Mexico in 600 years.

There are a thousand theories on the best way to go through pilot training. Each has pros and cons, but in my opinion, the "all or nothing" approach seems to be the most effective. This means a total commitment to Undergraduate Pilot Training on your part with no back-up plan or path. If you fail, you will literally have to start your career path over again.

Okay, here is the very last motivational thought I am going to tell you about earning your wings and becoming an Air Force pilot. If I can make it, you can make it. I come from a decidedly non-military family, a marginal Southern public education, and a totally non-aviation related criminal justice degree. I have always been an unenthusiastic (to put it mildly) academic student and virtually no talent when it comes to doing math in public. I began my Air Force career with a whopping three hours of flying time and that was riding in a Cessna 172 with a family friend. I have always said that I got through flight school by great friends, hard work, and the sure knowledge that I could make it. It is really just that simple, if I can make it, you can make it!

MERITOCRACY

What is one of the very best things about U.S. Air Force pilot training? Hands down it is because it is the last true meritocracy left alive in America today. The UPT program literally does not care about your sex, degrees, pedigrees, money, or fame. Everyone is equal in the eyes of the check pilot. All that matters is your performance, but also the reverse of the coin is true, your performance is all that matters--your performance determines your success or failure. It is all in your hands, literally.

You are being evaluated and graded on everything you do in Undergraduate Pilot Training. Every single test question, every single maneuver, and even your military bearing is meticulously scored and added to your electronic file. All those grades are placed into the Air Force's giant "Gonkculator" and you are rank ordered with your classmates. The better your score, the better choices you have when it is time to go to your follow-on aircraft. I will be honest, it gets old being under that powerful microscope for a solid year. At the same time, it is fantastic to be in an arena where your ability and hard work are rewarded. Let's face it--that just does not happen much in America anymore.

MY VERY BEST STUDENT

On paper, Mary was an unimpressive student pilot. She came to

Undergraduate Pilot Training with mediocre grades from a forgettable University, but that fluff hid an iron will and a desire to be the very best. When she arrived in the T-38 flight room and sat across from my desk, about the only thing that I noted was that her Southern accent was actually worse than mine. The first thing that jumped into my mind when I heard her speak was, "that thick of an accent yells to the world--no job and no education," a pure West Virginia drawl. Some of life's greatest surprises come from very unassuming packages and Mary was about as "unassuming, plain Jane" as they come.

Over the next six months, I and the other instructor pilots had our minds changed and she became the best student I have ever known.

In most respects, Mary was like every other student that came into the T-38 phase of flight school--enthusiastic and hard working. Her "hands" (the ability to put the jet in the time/place where you want it) while actually flying were good, but not exceptional. What truly set Mary apart was her drive to attack the program and make herself the best pilot she could be, not let the program push and pull her along. The difference sounds subtle but it is profound. In Mary's mind, it wasn't good enough to pass a particular block of training, she insisted on *mastering* each block of instruction and I now understand that drive is where "genius" lives. She was not afraid to say, "I did that instrument approach well enough to pass the ride but I want to do it better." She would ask for additional simulators or time during sorties to master the art of flying, not just meet the minimum standard. (The extra simulators and using time during a sortie is allowed, if you are progressing normally.) In that relentless drive to attain dominance in all aspects of aviation, she easily became a top performer in her class. It is clear to me now that Mary's performance in flight school is the picture perfect example of why UPT is designed the way it is. Pilot training is devised to reward the relentless, self-motivated student. The hallmark of this kind of character is the student that refuses to settle for "good enough" and pushes for excellence in every aspect of training.

In all honesty, Mary was a better student than I was and I am comfortable with that fact. I learned my lesson and have tried to copy her example every time I am back in training, even today.

Mary went on to finish flight school in fine style. She was snapped up by an airlift unit and has had an exceptional career as a professional aviator and leader. Best of all, I have had the honor and privilege to fly with her in some of the worst locations in the world and can attest to her outstanding airmanship and professionalism.

On a side note, I still owe Mary 25 minutes of T-38 flight time. Her last flight in the T-38 was scheduled to be a simple aerobatic sortie to complete her required flight hours in the final few days before her graduation. I was scheduled to fly with her and when I woke up that morning, I could tell I was coming down with something, but I didn't want to get off the flying schedule. We went through the normal preflight briefing, and I felt fine when we stepped to the jet. Once we got into the air, however, I went straight downhill. As she flew that T-38 to the absolute limit of its performance envelope, I sat in the back seat and tried to keep my breakfast down. I was progressively getting more sick and weak but Mary kept pulling high G-force maneuvers. It was hell on me and I needed to get on the ground because I was worried that I might pass out. The weather was a little borderline but certainly good enough for the profile we were flying. However, I wussed out and told her that I thought the weather was getting marginal and we needed to go back to the base and shoot some landing patterns. Once we recovered to the base, she shot one landing and I told her that I thought it was beginning to sleet (it wasn't) and that the next landing would be a full stop--the T-38 absolutely cannot operate in an icing environment. I knew Mary was pissed, but didn't say a word. We touched down with enough gas to fly for another 30 minutes, and her T-38 flying was officially over forever. She was going on to the C-5 cargo aircraft and would never fly high performance jets again. My wussiness cost her 25 minutes of glory and I have always felt bad about it. Mary and I are friends to this day and every once in awhile she reminds me of those 25 lost minutes.

Do you have the passion to follow the road less travelled?
Over the years, I have heard a myriad of reasons why people did not try or gave up trying to become a pilot without ever getting into an airplane. Here are a couple of examples:

I would have gone to flight school but I don't have perfect vision.
You do not have to have perfect vision to be a USAF pilot! It is so important that I will state it again; you do not have to have perfect vision to be an Air Force pilot. The standard is distant vision cannot exceed 20/200, near vision cannot exceed 20/40 and both correctable to 20/20--you are good to go.

I wanted to go to flight school but my guidance counselor told me I have to be a math (physics, engineering, Chinese) major to be a pilot.
Wrong! In order to get into flight school, you must pass the Air Force Officer's Qualifying Test (AFOQT). The AFOQT is very similar to the SAT and ACT with a few additional sections. Pass the test and score high enough in the pilot section, you clear that hurdle. Majoring in mathematics is not a requirement.

If I can make it, you can make it.
From the outside, United States Air Force Specialized Undergraduate Pilot Training (UPT) can look incredibly difficult to be accepted to and nearly impossible to complete. I have found that there is a tremendous amount of confusion and misperception about pilot training, and the myths cause people to give up on their dreams of becoming a pilot long before they take their first flight.

Years ago, as a freshman in college, I began my journey to flight school in an ROTC (Reserve Officers' Training Corps) classroom. The lecture hall where we were all assembled held about 100 people who were just starting the ROTC program. I will never forget when the instructor stood up and said, "Okay, who here is interested in becoming pilots?" Of the 100 people in the room, about 80 guys raised their hands. After four years of college and the screening process to get there, fourteen cadets graduated from the ROTC program and became Air Force officers. Only three of us had earned pilot training slots, and of those, two of us graduated from flight school--two out of eighty. Remember, these are just numbers--not the odds of making it to flight school. Your personal odds are 100% or 0%.

What amazed and frightened me was how easily people threw away their dreams. The vast majority of those people in the lecture hall did not get eliminated during the screening process, they individually decided to quit the process and chose not to pursue their dream. I sometimes wonder what kind of life those people lead today. Do you think their life is better or worse from that decision to quit?

"Be bold and mighty forces will come to your aid."
--Johann Goethe

Not long ago, I had to have some dental work done. The dental surgeon came into the room to explain to me how the procedure was going to be accomplished. In the course of our discussion it came out that I am an Air Force pilot. The dental surgeon, a fantastic professional who spent hundreds of thousands of dollars on his education and training, a man who owns his own practice and is a highly respected member of the community, stopped what he was doing and wanted to talk about flying--a lot. For the next half hour, this man wanted to discuss, in detail, my job and life. In the end, he mentioned about being an Air Force pilot, "That is the job I really wanted to do." The irony was not lost on me and should not be missed by you. Becoming an Air Force pilot is a long, challenging road and when you earn those silver wings, you command respect for the rest of your life.

Another truth is that the U.S. Air Force produces the finest pilots in the world and the reason why is because our training program is second-to-none. Strip away all the advanced aircraft, technology and our quality advantage in equipment and Air Force pilots will still win in combat, the product is that good. Air Force pilots are innovative, original, and overcome every obstacle you can throw at us. You might think to yourself that kind of statement is hyperbole, but over 25 years I have flown with pilots from virtually every country, culture, and background in the world. Hands down, we are the very best and our combat record proves that again and again. The United States literally wrote the book on airpower and the Air Force is the master of aerial warfare. With a little hard work, some physical attributes and an ounce of hand eye coordination, you can be one of us.

The bottom line on all of this discussion is simple. Becoming a United States Air Force pilot is a difficult but attainable goal. Tenacity and hard work can get you there, but it is all up to you.

If you are ready, let's get started!

OVERVIEW OF UPT

Before we get into the specifics of Undergraduate Pilot Training, it is important to give you an overview of the road to the silver wings and a frame of reference of the path ahead. To cover this time period, I will give you a quick 35,000-foot view of the entire path to and through flight school. Afterwards, I will break down each segment in detail and give you the intel and tricks of the trade to make the road easier. All this information is meant to remove the mystery of UPT and set you up for success in this once-in-a-lifetime opportunity.

The journey to a pair of silver, United States Air Force pilot wings begins with just you and your own thoughts and desires. Do you want this life? Whether it takes you two seconds or two years to answer this question honestly, only you can make this decision for yourself. It takes commitment and dedication from you to make it--think tenacity. There will be moments of abject humiliation, when you have done your absolute best and failed spectacularly. There will be times when you scare yourself witless in the airplane. Those times are counter balanced by the most wonderful moments in your entire life, like feeling your heart leap as you lead a formation of aircraft through a cloud layer and being bathed in the brilliant morning light as you clear the cloud deck. Or maybe the priceless moment as your name is called and you walk across the stage to receive your wings. These are the moments that make it all worthwhile, but only you can decide if it is worth the effort. Looking back over a 27-year aviation career I can tell you that it is, but I can't want it for you--the dedication has to come from you.

Let me assure you of this, do not try to become a pilot for someone else--you will fail or be completely miserable. I have flown with people who became pilots because their family was well meaning and turned the mental or financial screws on their children to become Air Force pilots. Those pilots either washed out (without much of a fight, I might add) or they were so wretched in their profession that they made everyone around them miserable. These are the pilots that bitch and complain about every single thing that is not perfect in their day and never take a moment to just enjoy the thrill of powered flight.

Once you make that commitment to attend pilot training, lock it in your heart and soul. This is the last time we will talk about wanting to become a pilot. You made the decision and now you are going to make the universe bend to your will to achieve your dream!

Think of pilot training as a pipeline. You may start the journey from many different and diverse backgrounds, enter the system through a specific gateway, go through the narrow section which is the pilot training process, and emerge as an Air Force pilot on the far end--going on to a variety of aircraft/assignments.

So, how long does this process actually take? From the day you make the commitment to become an Air Force pilot to the day you are flying operational missions varies greatly based on your education, availability of training, and simple timing. However, if every variable falls perfectly into place, the time you go from a college graduate to a fully operational F-16 pilot is about three years. Add in another 18 months of training once you arrive at your operational squadron and then you are ready to go to war. Bottom line, if all the stars align, you can be a fully trained, operational pilot in four to five years.

Here is the roadmap that takes you from point A to B.

First off, here is the laundry list of requirements to become an Air Force Officer and to qualify for a pilot training slot. We will discuss this list in much greater detail later.

- Be a United States citizen

- Be of good moral character (this is translated to mean, have a reasonably clean police record)

- Baccalaureate degree (any major is accepted)

- Meet the required Air Force Officer Qualifying Test (AFOQT) scores

- Earn a pilot slot

- Become a commissioned Air Force officer

- Pass the USAF flight physical

- Pass the USAF fitness assessment

- Begin pilot training by age 30

That is all that is required to be accepted into the Air Force and pilot training. It is not an easy bar to make but it is not impossible either. The best way to be accepted into the ranks of the Air Force is small efforts, every single day. Nobody is asking you to become a "warrior monk" who eats, sleeps, and lives 24/7 just to be a steely-eyed killer. First off, you will be boring as hell to be around and secondly, you will burn out long before you see the inside of a cockpit. Just plan on putting in a few hours a week toward achieving these items and you will do just fine. This is a highly competitive process and you have to work to make sure you have a strong application package, no matter if you go through Reserve Officers' Training Corps (ROTC), Officer Training School (OTS), or the Air Force Academy to get your commission. Remember, the Air Force wants you to succeed and become a pilot. Trust me when I tell you, the results are well worth the effort!

Once you have earned your pilot slot and commissioned as a second lieutenant, the train starts to pick up speed. Soon after commissioning, you will be assigned to one of the pilot training bases. In stereotypical military fashion, you get to request your preference of which UPT base you want to attend, and the Air Force will decide where you will go based on their needs and training availability. There are three main UPT bases--Vance AFB in Enid, Oklahoma; Columbus AFB in Columbus, Mississippi; and Laughlin AFB in Del Rio, Texas.

Additionally, pilot training is conducted at Sheppard AFB in Wichita Falls, Texas, and is the program that hosts the Euro-NATO (ENJJPT) program that trains our allied pilots in addition to American pilots. This program is geared toward training for the fighter pilot arena. Again, we will discuss this topic in some detail later.

No matter where you go to pilot training, arriving at your UPT base is literally stepping into another world. All day, every day, aircraft are moving. As you walk down the street you see T-6 Texan IIs in the break above your head, T-38s taxiing in formation for a departure, and T-1s making approaches. The typical pilot training base conducts as many take offs and landings as Chicago's O'Hare International Airport—every single day. Pilot training bases are intentionally placed in isolated areas so students and instructors can take full advantage of the wide-open airspace.

You will usually be offered unaccompanied officer's quarters (UOQ) on base to live in and the opportunity to get settled into your new life. Imagine a slightly larger, better dorm room from your college days, but the UOQs have the best feature of all--location, location, location. The Qs are located literally a few minutes' walk from the flightline, flight simulators, and academic classrooms.

Depending on class and training availability you may be placed into OAPT (Officers Awaiting Pilot Training) status. This usually happens when there will be a gap between the time you arrive on station and the date your pilot training class begins. This time can be anywhere from two to six months and frankly, it can be a very tedious time and will sorely try your patience. The Air Force will make full use of your high-dollar education by assigning you to a job on the base. It can be aggravating to see people you know start flight school and complete Phase II while you are working a 9-5 office job in the base housing office. You came here to fly and you are handing out towels at the gym; everyone knows it is frustrating!

The hidden benefit to being in OAPT status is that you are learning the "UPT system" through your buddies currently in flight school and getting a chance to study the important critical "must learn" data, without the pressure of actual flight training. The idea is to share knowledge with the OAPT mafia and get ready for UPT.

During this time you will be sent to Initial Flight Training (IFT), which is conducted in Pueblo, Colorado. (Unless you already have a private pilot's license.) This four-week program is designed to test your ability to learn to fly "the Air Force way" and give you a taste of the pace of actual pilot training. Flying the Diamond DA-20 aircraft, you will clock about 14 flight hours with a solo and checkride flights included. A civilian contracted company, Doss Aviation, runs this program. This program is discussed in detail in chapter five.

Wonder of wonders will occur and one day you will wake up and it is your "zero day," the beginning of Undergraduate Pilot Training! Undergraduate Pilot Training is a highly planned and executed 52-week program (55 weeks at ENJJPT) that is designed to take a person who has never flown before and turn them into an accomplished aviator. UPT is broken down into three phases.

Phase I is your indoctrination into the Air Force aviation system. The entire year can best be described as trying to drink water from a fire hose. Information is thrown at you from every direction and you have to determine what is critical and what can wait for later. You will be issued your uniforms for flying: flight suit (which you will spend most of your professional life wearing), flight boots, and the tons of publications that you are supposed to know yesterday. In addition, you get your first introduction to your classmates. You don't know it yet, but these guys and girls will be some of the greatest friends of your life.

Aerospace Physiology begins quickly (usually day three) and you are introduced to the effects of the flying environment on the human body. Parachute procedures, the hanging harness, and disconnecting as you are being dragged across the ground are all part of your routine. All this culminates in an altitude chamber ride and your first UPT academic test. The chamber ride is conducted in a heavy steel vault and the air pressure is reduced so that your body can experience the effects of high altitude on the human body.

For the final section of Phase I you are plunged into Undergraduate Pilot Training academics, big time. Long hours in the classroom and on the computer systems are the order of the day. To help focus your attention on academics you begin the many rounds of regular tests for each section of instruction. Added into the stress of Phase I is the sure knowledge that every day that passes is a day closer to the flightline and the T-6 Texan II.

Phase II arrives and everything you love and hate about UPT begins. 12-hour days are the standard and you are introduced to the crawl-walk-run process of Air Force flight instruction. You will be shown a particular way of doing every task in flying, for example; the aircraft walk-around inspection. The next day, you will be expected to do that walk around with the help and guidance of your instructor pilot (IP). Once you have learned that task to proficiency, you are expected to be able to do that, perfectly, from that day forward. Failure to complete the task properly in the future is called regression, and it is a bad thing.

Milestones in Phase II occur often and are memorable for the rest of your life: first flights, aerobatics, first solo flight and being tossed into the dunk tank by your classmates.

The fire hose of knowledge being shot at you is now in full force. Hours of preparation are required for each flight, and mastering the complexities of chairflying becomes your key to survival. Stress and mental exhaustion are your constant companions. Fellow classmates start buckling under the pressure and begin to wash out. Some smart-ass instructor will say the dreaded statement, "Just remember, you are only six rides away from being washed out of here." Academics are still in full force and you will finally come face-to-face with the hated reality of "Stand Up." This is the moment during the morning flight briefing when an instructor pilot describes an emergency situation in the aircraft, and then your heart freezes as your name is called. Your task is to stand up (hence the name), identify the problem, and explain how you will bring the emergency situation to a logical conclusion. Mess it up, you are publically embarrassed and pulled from the flying schedule for that day.

Just when you start to figure out the T-6 and the Air Force way of flying, you get to take your very first checkride. Mid-phase checkride is the culmination of all the studying and flying you have done so far. You will take your check pilot out for a standard sortie of aerobatics, takeoffs, and landings. If everything goes well, you keep progressing in the syllabus. Fail, and you start on the slippery slope of washing out. More classmates will disappear as they do not measure up or can't keep up with the pace of the program. These are the darkest days of the hardest training in the United States military.

Slowly and painfully, you begin to learn your new profession. You start to feel the freedom and utter joy of flight. All that studying begins to pay off as different pieces of knowledge all click together and the entire system starts to make sense. The routine of studying and chairflying comes together, and you no longer feel completely stupid in the air or on the ground. More and more tasks are introduced and mastered. The speeding train of Undergraduate Pilot Training is in full motion and up to speed--it has been hard to get on and now it is hard to get off. Final contact checkride comes and goes with more of your classmates eliminated from the program. Instruments and formation phases arrive and flying becomes the greatest thing imaginable! More checkrides and before you know it, you complete the T-6 phase and make it to track select.

Track select night occurs at the end of Phase II and it is a big party for everyone in the T-6 squadrons. You are called in front of everyone in a big auditorium and this is where the beauty of meritocracy is on display for God and the world. Your performance through every phase of pilot training is quantified, measured, and scored. Based on that ranking and your personal desires, you are "tracked" into either the T-38 or T-1 airframe. The T-38 track sets you on the path to be a fighter or bomber pilot, while the T-1 puts you in line for being a tanker or transport pilot.

Before you can even turn around, your class begins Phase III, and the final dash to your wings! As terrible as it sounds, everyone has to begin from square one in a brand new aircraft. Only now you have the benefit of knowing what to study and what is important right now.

It is the fire hose effect all over again as academics and new Bold Face/ Ops Limits tests become your new friends. This is really the snapshot of your future career in aviation, no matter where your path leads. Once you master a new technique, procedure, maneuver, or aircraft, the next challenge begins.

In the fighter/bomber track, the T-38C will introduce you to high-performance maneuvering and formation flying. Let me guarantee you that flying three feet away from another aircraft at 500 knots is an amazing experience. Mid-air rejoins and low-level navigation sorties are the order of the day.

Over in the T-1 world, the mysteries of the tanker/transport world are revealed. Advanced navigation, airdrop, and air refueling procedures become second nature to you.

Both tracks are designed to set you up for future success in your follow-on assignments. Each segment of the training has a real world application. Best of all, you will slowly see your instructors begin to step back and allow you to take more and more responsibility for your own training. Slowly but surely the light at the end of the tunnel begins to appear and you think that maybe, just maybe you might make it! More checkrides, more Stand Up and the pressure never seems to relent. You know that mathematically the odds are on your side for success, but the UPT grind continues on and on. Then suddenly, assignment night arrives and your blood pressure skyrockets. Finally, you and the world will know your next aircraft and the path your future will take! The hours and hours of agonizing over your "dream sheet" are about to pay off.

Assignment night is an even bigger party held at the base club and well-wishers come from far and wide to see where this pivot point in your life will take you. You awake that morning as a simple T-1 student pilot and that night you are a future C-17 pilot on your way to Hawaii--it is just that dramatic/scary/exciting. You hear your name called and stand before hundreds as your flight commander has a little fun at your expense, commenting on some of your less-than-stellar moments in pilot training. The music plays and on the screen you see your future airplane and in a twinkling, your life changes. Sometimes the moment is a dream fulfilled, sometimes it is a dream destroyed, but every time it is a realization that you are going to be a professional pilot. Assignment night occurs only a couple of weeks prior to graduation and the remaining time in UPT is a blur. Final flights and checkrides are the only hurdles left in the formal Undergraduate Pilot Training program. Once you have completed all the syllabus items, your biggest concern becomes all the family members that will arrive in town. People you hardly know or remember will all come out of the woodwork to share in your amazing achievement.

Believe it or not, graduation day will arrive. You put on your service dress uniform, the one you have not touched in a year since starting flight school. After the pomp, ceremony, and required speeches in all formal Air Force graduations, the moment you have worked for arrives. The announcer calls your name, follow on assignment, and hometown. You walk across the stage, are handed your silver wings, and shake the wing commander's hand. At that moment--you are now and will forever be, the very best of the best--an Air Force pilot!

GETTING TO PILOT TRAINING

COLLEGE GRADUATION TO COMMISSIONING

Specialized Undergraduate Pilot Training or SUPT (or really just UPT), is a highly planned and executed program that is designed to take a person from off the street with little to no flight experience and turn him/her into a world class aviator in 52 weeks while logging a mere 175 hours of flight time. You walk in the door a ground pounder, you walk out the door the envy of every air force in the world. Students arrive from all over the country with a wide variety of flight experience. I have seen veteran airline pilots and recent college graduates with just a few hours of total flight time enter UPT at the same time and all graduate. In the same vein, I personally witnessed civilian flight instructors with 3,000 hours of flight time fail spectacularly because they would not adapt to the "Air Force way" of flying. All of this is a testament to the Air Force's time-tested training program and to the skill and dedication of the instructor pilot corps, especially the First Assignment Instructor Pilots (FAIP). These superior pilots are the gatekeepers to the Air Force standard of excellence and the reason the USAF is second-to-none in the world. To get student pilots to this world-class level is due partly to a proven training system and mostly to the instructor pilots that implement the flying standards every single day.

Understanding the Undergraduate Pilot Training system and the Air Force's philosophy will make the entire process of how to become a pilot clearer.

SPECIALIZED UNDERGRADUATE PILOT TRAINING VS. UNDERGRADUATE PILOT

Training SUPT vs. UPT

Like all exceptional military training programs, Air Force pilot training adapts and changes over to time in order to fine-tune the finished product. A monumental change in flight school took place in the early 1990s with the introduction of the T-1 Jayhawk and Specialized Undergraduate Pilot Training (SUPT). This new program divides classes upon entering Phase III into two training tracks, the Tanker/Transport (T/T) track and the Fighter/Bomber (F/B) track. The students in the T/T track leave the T-6 program and go on to fly the T-1 Jayhawk, which resembles a small business jet, while the F/B track selects go on to fly the T-38 Talon.

The logic behind the decision is pretty sound: Why do you want to spend the money and wear on the old T-38 when some of the students who go on to fly transport or tanker aircraft will never fly in close formation? Also, why have fighter/bomber-bound students waste flying hours on learning advanced navigation procedures, which they will never use during their operational lives? The thought process goes: all USAF pilots can do those skills to some degree, but if you are going to spend training dollars, put those resources on future requirements/capabilities that you *know* will best serve the Air Force and the student.

In a nutshell, here is the laundry list you must meet in order to be accepted to pilot training. Be aware, requirements change all the time, so do your research and talk with recruiters so you have accurate information to make decisions. Make sure to do your own checking of the facts and double-check each item *on a regular basis.* I recommend you check them every few months for changes. You must meet these requirements:

- Be a United States citizen

- Have a reasonably clean police record

- Have a baccalaureate degree (any major is accepted)

- Meet the required Air Force Officer Qualifying Test (AFOQT) scores

- Earn a pilot slot

- Become a commissioned Air Force officer

- Pass the USAF flight physical

- Pass the USAF fitness assessment

- Begin pilot training by age 30

Trust me, this list sounds overwhelming, but by attacking it a little bit every day, it can be completed within a reasonable amount of time and effort. Besides, if the Air Force made it easy, it would not be worth it.

I have heard it said that to make a single Air Force pilot, it takes approximately 500 people that fall into the proper demographic. One in 500! Intelligence, tattoos (and their location), drug use, run-ins with the law, health issues, hearing, and eyesight are all just a handful of the reasons people never even get close to the inside of a jet. In order to bull through those hurdles, you have to have perseverance and determination. The one key word in this entire process is **tenacity**. Plenty of people will try to tell you "no," say you don't meet a requirement, or try to derail you onto another career path. You have to stay focused and driven every single day. No matter what the pilot manning numbers may say, there is always room in the Air Force for outstanding Air Warriors. Of all the hurdles in making it to zero day (the first day of flight school) *self doubt*--deciding that going to flight school is too high a bar for you and not even trying--eliminates far more people than all the other reasons combined.

"Our doubts are traitors, and make us lose the good we oft might win, by fearing to attempt."

William Shakespeare

Add in to this equation the attrition of washing out while actually in Undergraduate Pilot Training and it is easy to see why this becomes an exclusive club to join. Of the 500 in the given demographic, only one will walk across the stage and pin silver wings to their chest. Impressive company, indeed!

UPT Requirements

-Be a United States Citizen

Kind of an obvious requirement, but it has to be stated. You must be a U.S. citizen to become an Air Force officer and only officers can be Air Force pilots. Not a U.S. citizen? Get started on the process to become one, it is that simple. The day to start is yesterday.

(Reasonably) Clean Police Record

The actual verbiage states that to be an Air Force officer, you must be of good moral character and that generally equates to a relatively clean police record.

Although it seems a little silly to actually say it out loud, the Air Force is not going to let you handle multi-million dollar aircraft (with the capability to kill lots of people in a flash) if you cannot master your own passions. You are an adult, so do as you please, but a serious brush with the law, especially one involving drugs or alcohol, and you are done before you even get started. If it is really your dream to fly jets, then a little "nerdy" living is an easy price to pay in order to make your dreams come to life. My grandmother's reminder of "Nothing good ever happens after eleven o'clock" really comes into play here.

Bachelor's Degree

For better or worse, the United States Air Force requires all pilots to be officers, and to be an officer, you must have a bachelor's degree--a bachelor of arts or bachelor of science in any major. The Air Force owns the metal that you want to fly and they require a college degree to use those airplanes, so obviously your first step is to get that college degree. Since this requirement dovetails nicely with gaining a commission as an officer, two avenues of becoming an officer are intertwined with gaining the bachelor's degree, the United States Air Force Academy (USAFA) and the Reserve Officers' Training Corps (ROTC). Working through either of these programs while attending college is an excellent way to: earn your degree, learn about the Air Force itself, get your commission as an officer, and earn that coveted pilot slot!

Check with an Air Force recruiter because this requirement changes back and forth, but as I write this, online degrees are being accepted.

The AFOQT – Air Force Officer Qualifying Test

While you are getting your degree and going through the commissioning process, you will have a chance to take the Air Force Officer Qualifying Test (AFOQT). Before you can be an officer you must pass the AFOQT, but it is honestly no big deal. The test is very similar to the Scholastic Aptitude Test and covers the normal expected areas (math and verbal), but adds in pilot and navigation aptitude sections. Each question is multiple choice, with four or five possible answers. Expect to go through 11 subtests and if you don't know the answer, go ahead and guess--wrong answers do not hurt you. To become a pilot, the minimum scores are Verbal--15, Quantitative--10, and Pilot--25. The test itself is really not that difficult, and there are tons of books and online material to help you study. You can only take the test two times (with a minimum interval of six months in between), so make sure you set yourself up for success by studying hard, taking practice tests, and getting plenty of rest the night prior to test day. The test is really similar to the SAT and ACT. The higher the test score, the better your package will score when you are trying to earn that pilot slot.

Earn your Pilot Slot

Just because you get a commission as an Air Force officer does not mean you are automatically accepted into Undergraduate Pilot Training. The next step is to earn a pilot training slot, and these can be very competitive. Each commissioning source (USAFA, ROTC, OTS) has a particular method of selecting the individuals to attend flight school, but a universal measuring stick in all the sources of earning a commission is the Pilot Candidate Selection Method (PCSM) score. To arrive at this score, the Air Force takes three measureable elements--the pilot subsection of the AFOQT, the candidate's Test of Basic Aviation Skills (TBAS) score, and their civilian flight time total—and plugs these numbers into an "undisclosed" formula and arrives at a numerical score between 1-99.

Rumor has it that approved civilian flying time counts for 60% of this score. The higher the score, the more likely the candidate will graduate from Undergraduate Pilot Training and the better chance that candidate will earn a pilot slot.

The Test of Basic Aviation Skills (TBAS) is set up very similar to a video game. During the game, the pilot candidate is put through their paces with a variety of tests that measure motor reflexes, hand-eye coordination, and the ability to monitor multiple machine inputs. The test itself takes a little more than an hour and there is no way to study or prepare for it. Really, it is as simple as that and there are no tricks or techniques to increase your score other than to get a good night's sleep, listen to the directions, and get on with it!

This PCSM score is important in the pilot training slot selection process, so it is critical for you to learn the techniques to maximize the results.

Looking at the pilot slot allocation strictly by the numbers, far and away the Air Force Academy has the highest percentage--roughly 50% (400+) cadets--going on to pilot training.

ROTC, as a block, receives around 400 pilot training slots per year. The typical Reserve Officers' Training Corps detachment can expect to see 10-20% of the graduating seniors going on to UPT. Some ROTC detachments have a reputation of getting more pilot slots than others, so that might be a factor in choosing a particular university. Officer Training School (OTS) garners the lowest overall number with 100-150 of its graduates going on to pilot training. Further, OTS acts as a systemic "shock absorber" to the Air Force pilot pipeline. When there is a pilot shortage (like today) the Air Force can rapidly increase or decrease pilot production by an associated change in Officer Training School.

Suffice it to say you need an invitation to go to flight school and the pilot slot is that invitation. No matter which route you take to flight school, choose the pipeline that fits your lifestyle and personality the best--you will be happier in the long run.

COMMISSIONED AS AN AIR FORCE OFFICER

There are three ways to obtain an officer's commission in the U.S. Air Force--the United States Air Force Academy (USAFA), Reserve Officers' Training Corps (ROTC), and Officer Training School (OTS). Every time there is a pilot shortage, a barrage of know-it-all voices take to the internet to bemoan the "officer pilot only" rule. The normal refrain is usually centered around the, "if they would only let enlisted airmen fly, I would do anything to become a pilot and never complain about an assignment" train of thought. I won't personally wade into that debate, but suffice it to say that if you really want to be a pilot bad enough and the Air Force wants you to be an officer--become an officer.

Each avenue to the gold bars, ROTC, OTS, and the Academy all have their pluses and minuses and where you receive your commission really doesn't matter. Once I got commissioned and especially after I became a pilot, nobody asked me what my commissioning source was and honestly, nobody really cares. That is the glorious thing about the meritocracy of Undergraduate Pilot Training--it is all about performance! I was commissioned through ROTC, and obviously I have a certain bias to that particular route to the officer's commission. I thoroughly enjoyed my time in college, and Air Force ROTC was a big part of the fun. Additionally, ROTC did not take a tremendous amount of my time. The biggest advantages I noticed the Air Force Academy and Officer Training School graduates had over my fellow ROTC grads and myself was that they knew how to march in formation much better than ROTC cadets and really know how to wear their service dress uniform. Since they spent a lot of time getting yelled at about uniforms (and the Academy guys wore them every day for four years), it stands to reason that they would know all the tricks of the trade.

Additionally, Air Force Academy students had the added benefit of a free education and a clear look of what a career in the Air Force really looks like.

All the military details didn't really matter much because I wore my service dress uniform a grand total of three times while I was in flight school--zero day, the graduation ceremony of the class one year ahead of my class, and my class' graduation.

Remember, no matter where you are in life, Officer Training School is always an option. No matter if you are a recent college grad or someone who started a regular career and wants to live their dream of becoming an Air Force pilot, that opportunity is open to you now, today.

My advice is to take a look at all three options, talk to recruiters, pilots, ROTC instructors at universities and ALOs (Academy Liaison Officers) in your area and see which fits your lifestyle and situation best. The bottom line is that the commission is required to get in the front door, so go get a commission.

Be leery of Air Force recruiters--Overall, Air Force recruiters do an incredibly difficult job and are outstanding Airmen. Daily, they fill the Air Force ranks with fantastic individuals who answer our nation's call to duty. However, they may inadvertently end up giving you bad career advice and lead you down a path you do not want to go. As I graduated high school, I knew I wanted to fly and spoke

Although the Air Force Academy is a free education, I have heard it said by multiple Academy graduates when speaking about going to college there, "Yes, it was a $100,000 education, shoved up your ass--a nickel at a time." Yikes!

to a recruiter that visited my school. The recruiter tried really hard to get me to enlist right away as an Air Force aircraft mechanic. He told me that once I went to basic training and completed technical training school I could just transfer jobs and become a pilot. Wrong, wrong, wrong. I talked to a family friend that was a pilot and he set me straight, but I almost signed on the dotted line. With no real military background in my family, I didn't have all the information I needed to make an informed decision. I am positive this recruiter had plenty of pressure to fill aircraft mechanic slots, but his actions were borderline dishonest. Bottom line, do your homework, like reading this book, and *verify everything in writing* before signing **anything!** It is your life and career, so don't leave anything to chance.

PASS THE AIR FORCE FLIGHT PHYSICAL

Needless to say, this is the most complete physical you will have in your life. Every part of you will be poked, prodded, pulled, stuck, bled, recorded, and measured. Let me assure you, this process is no fun and you will not have a good time. But in the high-intensity environment of modern aerial combat, you have to be at absolute peak performance and that starts with being physically suited to the high stress demands of modern aviation. Anything less and we are just signing your death warrant.

The physical standards are very strict for pilot applicants:

1. Normal color vision

2. Uncorrected distant vision cannot exceed 20/200

3. Uncorrected near vision cannot exceed 20/40

4. Both distance and near vision must be correctable to 20/20 or better

5. Meet all the refraction and astigmatism requirements (read good eyes)

6. Corrective eye surgery could be a disqualifier!

7. No history of hay fever, asthma, or allergies after 12 years old

8. Standing height of 64-77 inches and sitting height of 34-40 inches

Be careful what you admit to and describe to the flight doctors. In certain instances, you may make a statement that seems innocent on the face of it but instantly eliminates you from pilot training.

For example:

Q. *Do you now or have you ever had frequent headaches?*

A. I had lots of headaches as a kid and my mom said I had migraines. After I turned 12, I never had another. Our family doctor figures I grew out of them.

What is the next word out of the flight doctor's mouth? "Next!"

That little exchange just eliminated you from USAF Undergraduate Pilot Training, period. Let's dissect the exchange and highlight the mistakes. Here is the problem: a migraine diagnosis is an instant disqualifier from being a pilot. Even though your mom is not a doctor, you admitted to something that may or may not be correct. Add in the family doctor statement and that *made* the migraine statement a medical fact. Now that you will not be going to UPT, what else were you planning to do for a career?

Here is how that entire exchange should have gone:
Q. Have you ever had frequent headaches?
A. No.

Am I being dishonest? No, because who is to say what "frequent" means? In my opinion, "frequent" means at least every day. The doctor may think that one headache per week is frequent. See the disconnect between the two viewpoints? Also, unless your mom, dad, second cousin, or whoever is actually a doctor, you do not have a diagnosis of a condition--and an opinion *is not a diagnosis!* A different way to say it is--unless a doctor examines you, conducts scientific tests, and treats you for a malady--**then you do not have an illness, allergy, or condition.** So many potential pilots kill their career by being too flippant and chatty at their flight physicals. Doctors are wonderful, hardworking Americans, but they are not your friends, and speaking too freely about your physical condition day-to-day is a recipe for disaster.

Especially dangerous words (in no particular order): allergy, migraine, hay fever, surgery, procedure, concussion, dizzy, head trauma, faint, heart murmur, arrhythmia, chest pain, color blindness, pass out, heart "anything," and knocked out.

The flight physical is a very demanding hurdle on your journey to the silver wings and there is very little you can actually do to improve your odds of passing successfully. The best way to help yourself over this obstacle is get a good night's sleep prior to the physical and keep your mouth shut--just my opinion.

PHYSICAL FITNESS BEFORE, DURING, AND AFTER UPT

You are joining the profession of arms and the sole focus of your future profession is winning our nation's war. To that end, you have to be ready physically to be plucked from your day-to-day life and deployed to hellish places. For some reason, wars in my lifetime have always been fought in really shitty locations. Afghanistan and Iraq are ridiculously hot in the summer, both easily reach 120 degrees. Afghanistan has the added bonus of being bone-rattling cold in the wintertime. The term "fighting season" takes on a whole new meaning when the winter grips the Khyber Pass. Wherever our nation sends us to fight next, rest assured it will not be pleasant. Aside from being sent to crappy places, you are expected to perform at the very highest levels in your chosen profession.

That is why you must establish and maintain a reasonable level of physical fitness throughout your flying career and if you set the right foundation, it will become your lifestyle.

Here are the things to remember when it comes to physical training: balance and common sense. You are not joining the Navy SEALS or Special Forces with the physical requirements those guys go through. Your duties will not require you to ruck 50 miles or excel at a Navy "Hell Week." The Air Force does not work that way. However, (there is always a catch) you can go from sitting comfortably in your aircraft to literally fighting for your life in a survival situation in the blink of an eye. You could be placed in every conceivable environment known to man. Open ocean, desert, mountain, and jungle terrain are all on the menu. Worst of all, add in the option that you could land in your own corner of hell with the enemy and they will be none-too-pleased that you just dropped bombs on them. They might be looking for a little payback and getting their hands on you so they can play the "punching bag game" with you is not a good idea. Don't think that all you need to do is sit quietly beside your jet and wait for a friendly helicopter to swoop in, pick you up, and whisk you away to safety. I have been told in real world mission briefings that, in certain operations, if I ditched the jet, I would need to walk 30+ miles through hostile territory for rescue. All I am saying is this--the Air Force standard of fitness is pretty simple, be fit enough to pass the fitness assessment on any given day and if you are forced to depart the aircraft, make sure you can save yourself in a survival situation.

The Air Force requirement for physical fitness is easy to achieve and honestly, you have no reason not to score an "Excellent" every time you take it. You will not be allowed to start UPT without a passing fitness score, so get on it. Additionally, you will be given two fitness assessments while you are at pilot training. Bust either one and you are telling the system that you are not really serious about being here.

The Fitness Assessment consists of:

• **Waist measurement**--This area has the most amount of heartburn for the average person. Basically, you step into a private area and pull up your shirt and the person giving the test pokes your side to find the top of your hipbone (the big brain people call it the superior border of the iliac crest). You then turn slowly while the proctor rolls out the tape. This phase is worth 20% of your score. Guys, if your gut measures more than 39 inches, you bust. Ladies, it is 36 inches for you.

• **Push-ups and Sit-ups** (or crunches, depending how you describe the movement), maximum amount in one minute--There are plenty of YouTube videos and workout programs that describe these exercises online, so look them up. Each exercise is worth 10% each of your total score and there is no excuse for not maxing them out. Also, there are no rest periods during these exercises, so if you take a breather in the wrong body position, you bust.

• Want to get really good at push-ups and sit-ups? Get off your ass and practice push-ups and sit-ups!

• **1.5 mile timed run**--Run from here to there in the required time and you win. This counts for 60% of the total score. There are more failures in the run than in any other area. Don't step off the track during the run or (you guessed it!) you bust. Don't think that since you are on the elliptical trainer for an hour every day you can pass the run portion of the test. I have witnessed over a thousand tests, and by far the biggest reason people fail is because they do not practice, especially the run.

Bust any individual part of the test and you bust the whole thing. Also, be aware that it is physically possible to make a passing score in each component but score so low overall that you fail the test.

Cardiorespiratory Endurance

Run Time (mins:secs)	Health Risk Category	Points
≤ 9:12	Low-Risk	60.0
9:13 - 9:34	Low-Risk	59.7
9:35 - 9:45	Low-Risk	59.3
9:46 - 9:58	Low-Risk	58.9
9:59 - 10:10	Low-Risk	58.5
10:11 - 10:23	Low-Risk	57.9
10:24 - 10:37	Low-Risk	57.3
10:38 - 10:51	Low-Risk	56.6
10:52 - 11:06	Low-Risk	55.7
11:07 - 11:22	Low-Risk	54.8
11:23 - 11:38	Low-Risk	53.7
11:39 - 11:56	Low-Risk	52.4
11:57 - 12:14	Low-Risk	50.9
12:15 - 12:33	Low-Risk	49.2
12:34 - 12:53	Moderate Risk	47.2
12:54 - 13:14 #	Moderate Risk	44.9
13:15 - 13:36 *	Moderate Risk	42.3
13:37 - 14:00	High Risk	0
14:01 - 14:25	High Risk	0
14:26 - 14:52	High Risk	0
14:53 - 15:20	High Risk	0
15:21 - 15:50	High Risk	0
15:51 - 16:22	High Risk	0
16:23 - 16:57	High Risk	0
≥ 16:58	High Risk	0

Body Composition

AC (inches)	Health Risk Category	Points
≤ 32.5	Low-Risk	20.0
33.0	Low-Risk	20.0
33.5	Low-Risk	20.0
34.0	Low-Risk	20.0
34.5	Low-Risk	20.0
35.0	Low-Risk	20.0
35.5	Moderate Risk	17.6
36.0	Moderate Risk	17.0
36.5	Moderate Risk	16.4
37.0	Moderate Risk	15.8
37.5 #	Moderate Risk	15.1
38.0	Moderate Risk	14.4
38.5	Moderate Risk	13.5
39.0 *	Moderate Risk	12.6
39.5	High Risk	0
40.0	High Risk	0
40.5	High Risk	0
41.0	High Risk	0
41.5	High Risk	0
42.0	High Risk	0
42.5	High Risk	0
43.0	High Risk	0
≥ 43.5	High Risk	0

Muscle Fitness

Push-ups (reps/min)	Points	Sit-ups (reps/min)	Points
≥ 67	10.0	≥ 58	10.0
62	9.5	55	9.5
61	9.4	54	9.4
60	9.3	53	9.2
59	9.2	52	9.0
58	9.1	51	8.8
57	9.0	50	8.7
56	8.9	49	8.5
55	8.8	48	8.3
54	8.8	47	8.0
53	8.7	46 #	7.5
52	8.6	45	7.0
51	8.5	44	6.5
50	8.4	43	6.3
49	8.3	42 *	6.0
48	8.1	41	0
47	8.0	40	0
46	7.8	39	0
45	7.7	38	0
44 #	7.5	37	0
43	7.3	36	0
42	7.2	35	0
41	7.0	34	0
40	6.8	33	0
39	6.5	32	0
38	6.3	31	0
37	6.0	30	0
36	5.8	≤ 29	0
35	5.5		
34	5.3		
33 *	5.0		
32	0		
31	0		
30	0		
29	0		
28	0		
27	0		
26	0		
25	0		
24	0		
23	0		
22	0		
21	0		
20	0		
19	0		
18	0		
≤ 17	0		

NOTES:

Health Risk Category = low, moderate or high risk for current and future cardiovascular disease, diabetes, certain cancers, and other health problems

Passing Requirements - member *must* : 1) meet minimum value in each of the four components, *and* 2) achieve a composite point total ≥ 75 points

* Minimum Component Values
Run time ≤ 13:36 mins:secs / Abd Circ ≤ 39.0 inches
Push-ups ≥ 33 repetitions/one minute / Sit-ups ≥ 42 repetitions/one minute

Target Component Values
Member should attain or surpass these to achieve ≥ 75.0 composite score

Composite Score Categories
Excellent ≥ 90.0 pts / Satisfactory = 75.0 - 89.9 / Unsatisfactory < 75.0

USAF Fitness Test Scoring /Males < 30 years of age

Cardiorespiratory Endurance

Run Time (mins:secs)	Health Risk Category	Points
≤ 10:23	Low-Risk	60.0
10:24 - 10:51	Low-Risk	59.9
10:52 - 11:06	Low-Risk	59.5
11:07 - 11:22	Low-Risk	59.2
11:23 - 11:38	Low-Risk	58.9
11:39 - 11:56	Low-Risk	58.6
11:57 - 12:14	Low-Risk	58.1
12:15 - 12:33	Low-Risk	57.6
12:34 - 12:53	Low-Risk	57.0
12:54 - 13:14	Low-Risk	56.2
13:15 - 13:36	Low-Risk	55.3
13:37 - 14:00	Low-Risk	54.2
14:01 - 14:25	Low-Risk	52.8
14:26 - 14:52	Low-Risk	51.2
14:53 - 15:20	Moderate Risk	49.3
15:21 - 15:50 #	Moderate Risk	46.9
15:51 - 16:22 *	Moderate Risk	44.1
16:23 - 16:57	High Risk	0
16:58 - 17:34	High Risk	0
17:35 - 18:14	High Risk	0
18:15 - 18:56	High Risk	0
18:57 - 19:43	High Risk	0
19:44 - 20:33	High Risk	0
≥ 20:34	High Risk	0

Body Composition

AC (inches)	Health Risk Category	Points
≤ 29.0	Low Risk	20.0
29.5	Low Risk	20.0
30.0	Low Risk	20.0
30.5	Low Risk	20.0
31.0	Low Risk	20.0
31.5	Low Risk	20.0
32.0	Moderate Risk	17.6
32.5	Moderate Risk	17.1
33.0	Moderate Risk	16.5
33.5	Moderate Risk	15.9
34.0 #	Moderate Risk	15.2
34.5	Moderate Risk	14.5
35.0	Moderate Risk	13.7
35.5 *	Moderate Risk	12.8
36.0	High Risk	0
36.5	High Risk	0
37.0	High Risk	0
37.5	High Risk	0
38.0	High Risk	0
38.5	High Risk	0
39.0	High Risk	0
39.5	High Risk	0
≥ 40.0	High Risk	0

Muscle Fitness

Push-ups (reps/min)	Points	Sit-ups (reps/min)	Points
≥ 47	10.0	≥ 54	10.0
42	9.5	51	9.5
41	9.4	50	9.4
40	9.3	49	9.0
39	9.2	48	8.9
38	9.1	47	8.8
37	9.0	46	8.6
36	8.9	45	8.5
35	8.8	44	8.0
34	8.6	43	7.8
33	8.5	42 #	7.5
32	8.4	41	7.0
31	8.3	40	6.8
30	8.2	39	6.5
29	8.1	38 *	6.0
28	8.0	37	0
27 #	7.5	36	0
26	7.3	35	0
25	7.2	34	0
24	7.0	33	0
23	6.5	32	0
22	6.3	31	0
21	6.0	30	0
20	5.8	29	0
19	5.5	28	0
18 *	5.0	27	0
17	0	26	0
16	0	25	0
15	0	24	0
14	0	23	0
13	0	≤ 22	0
12	0		
11	0		
10	0		
9	0		
8	0		
≤ 7	0		

NOTES:

Health Risk Category = low, moderate or high risk for current and future cardiovascular disease, diabetes, certain cancers, and other health problems

Passing Requirements - member *must*: 1) meet minimum value in each of the four components, *and* 2) achieve a composite point total ≥ 75 points

* Minimum Component Values
Run time ≤ 16:22 mins:secs / Abd Circ ≤ 35.5 inches
Push-ups ≥ 18 repetitions/one minute / Sit-ups ≥ 38 repetitions/one minute

Target Component Values
Member should attain or surpass these to achieve ≥ 75.0 composite score

Composite Score Categories
Excellent ≥ 90.0 pts / Satisfactory = 75.0 - 89.9 / Unsatisfactory < 75.0

USAF Fitness Test Scoring /Females < 30 years of age

PHYSICAL FITNESS TO BLOW OFF STEAM

Build this good habit pattern and you will be grateful the rest of your life, sweat at least six times a week! I can't hammer this point hard enough. Pilot training is 52 weeks of constant stress and anxiety. The everyday level of increased stress is bad enough and then there are the peak, hyper-stressful times of checkrides and academic tests. There are plenty of studies that confirm the obvious--being in good shape will allow you to fight off the stress and allows you to perform at your best. We all know how a good run or workout makes us feel better after a crappy day. I won't even go into the long-term benefits of being in shape and keeping you healthy, hence *on the flying schedule*. Come to pilot training in good shape, maintain a workout program while on station to help manage your stress level, and going forward, keep a body ready to go to war. This is an easy one and something you can start today--get off your ass and get cracking.

BEGIN PILOT TRAINING BY AGE 30

Another somewhat obvious requirement, but flying is a game for the young. I have lived through some ass kicking 24-hour duty days in the C-5 and the G-forces in the fighter aircraft are nothing short of incredible. High tempo flight operations are truly a younger person's game. If you want to be a pilot, clear the crap out of your life and your head. Ditch the dead end, soul-killing job and take a shot at your dream. Figure out a path to get to Undergraduate Pilot Training and get it done. Don't look back at 31 years old and say, "I wish I would have gone to flight school." I literally hear that every week from regular civilians, so don't miss your chance by waiting until it is too late. As a safe rule of thumb, get started on this journey by your 27th birthday.

EVERYTHING IS WAIVERABLE

Tenacity--you will hear that word over and over again when discussing pilot training. At its heart, it means the dogged pursuit of your goal (dreams) despite the roadblocks placed in front of you. The more desirable the goal, the bigger and tougher the roadblocks will seem. At times, it will appear that the entire system is locked and loaded to prevent you from getting to flight school. That said, here is a little secret the system will not bother to tell you – **almost everything on this list is waiverable.** This means that if you don't qualify because of a particular reason, it is possible the Air Force will grant you a waiver for your issue and let you attend Undergraduate Pilot Training. The two notable exceptions to this rule are U.S. citizenship and color blindness. (It does stand to reason that if you mistake the color of a light in an aircraft that it could lead to tragic problems.)

Additionally, there are multiple ways that waivers can be granted, through multiple organizations. Trust me on this, I have seen the process up close and the persistent person can win.

Here is an example how the wavier system works:

Let's say you had a brush with the law when you were in junior high, nothing serious, just a simple misdemeanor that was handled at the local level. You have kept yourself on the straight and narrow ever since.

Somewhere along your journey to flight school, perhaps the security background check, the police record is flagged. When the information is returned to the recruiter, he sadly informs you that the Air Force has a new policy and no pilot candidates can have a conviction of any type on their records. A less knowledgeable person would give up right there, but you read this book and know that **everything is waiverable!**

The next words out of your mouth should be, "Who is the waiver authority and how do I go about submitting a package?" This is Air Force speak for *who can grant me a permission slip for this problem and in what format do I have to make the request for the waiver?*

If the recruiter (or whoever is guiding your application process) does not want to help or does not know how, very politely ask to speak to the next level of authority-- and again and again--until you get someone who can help you.

If for some reason your waiver is denied, keep going to a higher level of authority. Keep plugging away, the system will work if you are tenacious. Very, very rarely does "no" actually mean no. Every time you are denied, ask very politely what the next step is in the process.

If, for some reason, you truly hit the end of the road and your waiver is denied,

COL. JAMES R. LACKEY

do not give up! The Air Force Reserve and the Air National Guard all have their own individual systems. Each step in this process can be repeated again (and again) and in the end all you have is one person to agree with your case.

No matter the issue, work the system and get that waiver. Remember, **everything is waiverable!**

THE AIR FORCE RESERVE AND THE AIR NATIONAL GUARD VS. ACTIVE DUTY

Two often overlooked organizations that fly top-of-the-line Air Force aircraft and are equally vital to the national defense are the Air Force Reserve and the Air National Guard. Either organization may be the right fit for you, the differences between them and the active duty Air Force is subtle, but profound.

The Air Force Reserve is a federally controlled element of the Air Reserve Component (ARC) and serves as backup to the active duty Air Force. The Reserve flies virtually all variants of the aircraft in the inventory. In some instances, the Air Force Reserve "owns" its own aircraft (unit equipped) and sometimes it shares planes with an active duty unit (active associate). Either way, the key factor is the Reserve is a federally (read Washington D.C.) controlled force.

The Air National Guard is a state-controlled element of the ARC. The Air Guard is primarily controlled by the individual state's governor and the running joke is to ask why does a state need their own Air Force? Most Air Guard units own their own aircraft.

Both the Air Force Reserve and the Air National Guard recruit and send their own pilot candidates to flight school. This fact may fit your particular situation. This means you can interview with the unit, be "hired" and sent to flight school knowing exactly the aircraft you will be flying. If this fits your personal situation and you are driven to fly a particular aircraft, get busy and check out which units of the Guard and Reserve fly in your area or the specific aircraft you want. Call the base, get the phone number of the pilot section and ask to speak to the Chief Pilot or the person in charge of hiring new pilots. Once you find the right person, ask them the process for submitting a package as a pilot. The requirements for being a commissioned Air Force officer and passing the flight physical are the same in the Guard and Reserve. As you have learned--do not accept "no" as an answer! A word of warning, the Reserve and especially the Air Guard can be a bit of a "good old boys" club, so it can be a long and difficult process to gain a pilot slot. Look at it from their point of view: they are hiring a pilot that they will be stuck with for the next 20+ years. The unit just wants to make sure they hire a good dude/dudette that they will not want to kill if they have to live with them in a tent for six months.

INITIAL FLIGHT TRAINING OR PRIVATE PILOT'S LICENSE

Initial Flight Training (IFT) is a four-week, flight-training program that is modeled on Undergraduate Pilot Training. Doss Aviation, a civilian contractor, runs the operation out of the Pueblo, Colorado, airport. Candidates are normally sent to IFT a couple of months prior to UPT and are given a glimpse into the Air Force method of flight instruction. The program includes a checkride and there is a chance the candidate could wash out.

If you have a FAA private pilot's license, you do not have to attend IFT and here in lies the question--should you plan to go to IFT or spend the money and time to get your private pilot's license?

I recommend going to Initial Flight Training, even though there is a chance you could wash out. The opportunity to get an Air Force designed experience makes the training worth the possibility of washing out.

I will discuss IFT in more detail later in the book.

THE JUMP WINGS DEBATE

Earning jump wings, or more accurately, the U.S. Army Basic Parachutist Badge, is an opportunity that may be offered to you prior to entering Undergraduate Pilot Training. There are two schools for earning this badge--either the U.S. Army's Airborne School at Fort Benning, Georgia, or the Air Force's Free Fall School located at the Air Force Academy in Colorado Springs. The upside to this training is that you can wear the jump wings on your uniform for the rest of your career. In fact, this is an approved badge to wear on your flightsuit's Velcro nametag.

To graduate from Army Airborne School, you must accomplish four daylight and one night drop. The school is three weeks in length and divided into Ground Week, Tower Week, and Jump Week.

The Air Force Academy's basic free-fall course or Airmanship 490 (AM-490) is focused more on free-fall parachuting with a more advanced, steerable parachute than what is used in the Army's jump school. Again, a total of five jumps are required to earn the badge.

As a side note, although you may complete the training from the USAFA free fall school, this does not qualify you to be in an operational jump unit--i.e., special operations. Only by graduating from Army Airborne School are you officially Airborne trained and qualified to jump in an operational unit.

There has been a long debate whether or not it is a good idea to attend jump school if your career path is to be a pilot.

The pro-jump school camp generally falls into the "develop character, confidence, and courage" discussion. There is some validity there and plenty of outstanding pilots have attended jump training. I can understand the pull to attend jump school and get that badge. In college, you spend a lot of time doing things that don't seem to have anything to do with living your dream of becoming a pilot. Jump school is offered right at this time and seems like the next best thing to flight school. In fact, I was *exactly* in that position. When I was in ROTC, applications were being accepted for Army Airborne School during my junior year. I got my application together and was ready to submit it. I was called to the detachment commander's office where I was told to forget jump school. "Lackey," he said, "if you go to jump school and fuck up your leg, you won't go to flight school and you will be worthless to everybody. Get out of my office." That was that, he wasn't going to even submit my package to compete for a slot. I was pissed and muttered a lot under my breath, but really there was nothing I could do about it. I wanted to be a pilot and if I pissed off the commander, he could ruin that dream with a phone call. I sucked it up and went about my business. The commander's reasoning was sound and looking back over 30 years, I totally agree with him.

You can do as you please, but I advise not taking the chance by attending jump school. Before going any further, let me clearly state that I have flown with plenty of outstanding pilots over the years with jump wings. I will also state that jump wings do not make you a better pilot, nor do they help you graduate from UPT. My main objection to jump wings is the potential for injury severe enough to eliminate you from the physical requirements of flight school. Jump out of a perfectly good airplane and wrap your leg around your head, no flight school for you.

I will state it bluntly: the risk of injury simply does not justify the gain of having a badge to wear. Napoleon commented that a soldier would fight long and hard for a little piece of colored ribbon and I believe that there is an element to this when it comes to jump wings.

Why are you reading this book? To give you the added knowledge in order to graduate from U.S. Air Force flight school and earn your pilot wings--everything else is a waste of time.

Getting your jump wings is not a mark of how dedicated you are to becoming a pilot and it does not get you closer to the silver wings

YOUR ONLINE LIFE

This area is not so much for flight school but more for your future as an American Warrior.

Get rid of your online life and delete as much as you can from past postings. If, God forbid, you are ever captured sometime in the future, you are giving your captors a world of free information about your private life. The last thing you want is to be interrogated by someone who knows all the intricate details of your private world. Worse, you are putting your loved ones at risk. The nature of warfare has changed, forever. There are no front lines and anyone is now a target.

When you have a large online presence and you send birthday wishes to your grandma, you just made her a possible target for the next jihadi crazy. Keep your private life, well, private.

So, when you look at the laundry list of requirements to become an Air Force officer and earn a pilot training slot, are you challenged or dejected? From the beginning, I have repeatedly stated that becoming an Air Force pilot is a long and difficult journey but absolutely worth the effort. I will be honest, the list looks long and complex but remember, no one is expecting you to finish it in a day, week, or month. You reach your goal by working on it slowly, step by step, for about a couple hours per week. When in doubt, work harder. Get it done and get that pilot slot!

FROM COMMISSIONING TO ZERO DAY

After graduation from college and commissioning as an Air Force officer, it can be weeks or months before you actually begin Undergraduate Pilot Training. It is not the time to goof off! These precious months are golden opportunities that you must use to prep for flight school. Every day that goes by, you are one day closer to Zero Day and you need to be ready to hit UPT will all the energy and focus you can manage. From the very first day of pilot training, you are being graded and in this meritocracy, performance is everything. How pissed off are you going to be if some jerk in your class gets that F-22 you wanted simply because he or she was more prepared for UPT than you were?

Sound, logical groundwork is the key to success so follow the steps I am going to outline and you will be good to go.

Remember this, from the time you are commissioned as an officer in the United States Air Force until the moment you walk across the stage and are pinned as an Air Force pilot, the USAF has spent a relatively small amount of money on you. If, during this time period, you step out of line in any meaningful way, the Air Force, as an institution, has very little problem with tossing you out on your ear. You are not an asset to the team (yet), the government has very little invested in you, and there are plenty of other people waiting to take your place. The philosophy is simple, it is far better to toss out the bad apples early and remove all the potential discipline problems than to try and rehabilitate those problem children once we have spent millions on their training. Adultery, conduct unbecoming of an officer, and driving under the influence are all clean kills that eliminate newly minted second lieutenants every year.

ENJJPT vs. SUPT

In the early 1970s the Air Force and NATO realized the need to increase the pilot training and interoperability between the United States and our European allies. To meet this requirement, ENJJPT was formed at Sheppard Air Force Base, Texas. ENJJPT stands for Euro-NATO Joint Jet Pilot Training.

The main differences between ENJJPT and SUPT lie more in program philosophies than in the actual substantive differences in the respective training syllabuses.

Some of the differences include:

- ENJJPT is scheduled for 55 weeks vs. 52 weeks for SUPT

- ENJJPT does not have a T-1 program, only T-38

- ENJJPT classes have a roughly 50-50 split between NATO students and U.S.

- Instructor pilots at Sheppard are from both our NATO allies and the U.S. Air Force. It is possible to have European pilots as your primary instructor pilots during your training

- The ENJJPT syllabus is more focused on formation (both two-ship and four-ship) and fighter fundamentals than the regular UPT syllabus

While regular SUPT is a broad program that is aimed at filling any cockpit in the Air Force, ENJJPT has a fighter focus--hence the lack of a T-1 option. If you have to boil it all down to one sentence--ENJJPT is in the business of making fighter pilots for the United States and our NATO allies. Because of this and the allure of being a fighter pilot, slots at ENJJPT are more competitive than for the regular UPT bases.

Which program is best for you? Like virtually every question that arises about careers, the answer is--it depends. In general, if your life's dream is to become a fighter pilot and this is an all-or-nothing commitment to you, then Sheppard might be the best path for you.

Myth--Attending ENJJPT guarantees you a fighter.
Fact--Although you may attend ENJJPT, you may not have the skillset to survive in the fighter arena. The T-38 track is "universally assignable"-- which means you can be assigned to any USAF aircraft.

There is another school of thought that goes like this--since all the really strong pilot training candidates will be trying to earn ENJJPT slots, why not go to regular UPT and be the #1 person in that class? It is easier to be #1 at Columbus AFB than #1 at Sheppard AFB. I am totally against this philosophy! Over the years, I have seen plenty of people play the "numbers game" and try to "game" the system. To be honest, occasionally it works, but when "working the system" fails, it fails spectacularly. Be warned, there is some truth in the old saying--*too clever by half.*

Realize, even if you work hard to get an ENJJPT slot and end up going to regular SUPT, it is not a failure on your part. The slots to Sheppard are very competitive and remember, the ultimate goal is to become an Air Force pilot. Use that disappointment to fuel your motivation--if the Air Force sends you to SUPT, hammer that program and be the #1 person in your class, that will show them!

Finally, after all is said done, this book is all about getting through flight school and earning your Air Force pilot wings. Whether you go to ENJJPT or SUPT, the information is universal to USAF pilot training and will make the difficult road a little easier.

AIR FORCE BASES FOR SUPT AND ENJJPT

There are three bases for Specialized Undergraduate Pilot Training

Vance AFB, Columbus AFB and Laughlin AFB, and the aforementioned Sheppard AFB for ENJJPT.

Through the decades of training pilots, the Air Force has determined that a parallel, three-runway configuration works best for training student pilots. Additionally, all the bases have access to an auxiliary airfield where additional takeoffs, landings and pattern work can be conducted in the T-6 Texan.

All four bases use three primary runways and they are usually utilized by having the T-6 operations on the shortest runway (usually closest to the main base), T-1 and T-38 departures on the center runway and T-38 operations primarily on the outside runway. I know this sounds complex, but it will make perfect sense when you begin flying.

Here is a quick look at the individual bases. This is not meant to be comprehensive, just a blurb about the reputation of the bases. There is plenty of information online about each base. Also, it is like that old joke-- what is your #1 pilot training base? The one they assign you!

Take a look at the money, time and effort placed on multiple runways and traffic patterns at pilot training bases. If the Air Force puts that kind of resources behind anything, then the AF thinks it is important. If the Air Force thinks takeoff, landings, and traffic pattern operations are that important, it makes sense for you to focus your initial study efforts into those areas.

VANCE AIR FORCE BASE

Located a few miles south of Enid, Oklahoma, Vance AFB happens to be one of the smallest bases in the United States. It is about 90 miles northwest of Oklahoma City, which means lots of farms, cattle, and oil. That kind of open range--read no trees--makes it the perfect place for flying operations. The thing to remember about Oklahoma is that the wind blows all the time. No kidding, all the time. The biggest redeeming factor of that kind of wind, it makes the best pilots in the world--in my humble opinion. Once you learn how to fly in that OK wind, you will never be intimidated

49

by challenging wind conditions ever again in your career.

Another nice aspect of Vance is the fact that pilot training is the primary mission. With no other formal schools or programs that will suck away resources, all the agencies on base pull in the same direction to accomplish the mission of making new pilots.

COLUMBUS AIR FORCE BASE

Located just north of Columbus, Mississippi, Columbus AFB has been a pilot training base on and off over the years. Occasionally a B-52 base, occasionally a pilot training field, Columbus enjoys the weather benefits of the South. Heat, humidity and thunderstorms all add up to make the Columbus grads some of the best Instrument Flight Rules (IFR) pilots in the Air Force. Clouds and the high humidity reduce the visibility, so even normal VRF flying is a challenge.

As far as a place to be stationed, Columbus has a lot going for it. Southern charm by the locals and there are plenty of colleges nearby make it a good place for your off time. A big plus is that Atlanta is just up the road for long weekends and all this adds up to a solid location to be in UPT.

LAUGHLIN AIR FORCE BASE

Close to the Mexican border in south Texas, Laughlin AFB is easily the most remote of the pilot training bases. The city of Del Rio is located just a few miles from the base, with San Antonio 150 miles to the east. South Texas weather is a major plus to training at Laughlin. Long stretches of clear skies and great flying weather make Laughlin ideal for flight school. Having San Antonio more than two hours up the road keeps the temptation of going there every weekend to a minimum. Finally, Lake Amistad is nearby and provides plenty of distraction during your off time.

SHEPPARD AIR FORCE BASE

Sheppard AFB is located near Wichita Falls in north central Texas. Aside from the ENJJPT program, Sheppard is also home to several Air Force technical schools. These schools are where enlisted airmen learn their specific Air Force careers before being sent to their world-wide bases. Flying operations at Sheppard are solid with few weather concerns. Due to the Euro-NATO training mission, Sheppard does not have T-1 training which makes the base similar to the classic AF pilot training bases of a generation ago, where you train in the primary trainer (in this case the T-6) and go on to the advanced trainer (the T-38).

Additionally, Dallas is driving distance east of Wichita Falls for long weekends.

Officers Awaiting Pilot Training (OAPT) or "Casual Students"

A big change since my time in pilot training involves Officers Awaiting Pilot Training (OAPT) or Casual Students. Casual students are officers that have graduated from college, been commissioned as lieutenants, and are awaiting the start of their pilot training class. The Air Force brings these officers to their pilot training base and has them begin working in support jobs around the base while they wait for their pilot training class to begin. Due to budget constraints and training issues, this period can be anywhere from one week to six months. For the OAPT'er, it can be frustrating to watch airplanes in the traffic pattern overhead every day as they walk back and forth to a pretty mundane office job.

Once you arrive at your pilot training base and complete inprocessing, expect to be assigned as a casual student to an office on station. You will not be given a whole lot of choice in the matter about where you are assigned but if you have an interest in a certain location or mission, certainly try and get placed there or swap with another OAPT who wants a change. Very few of these jobs have a direct relation to flying but it never hurts to ask.

During this time, you will have the chance to get settled on base and set up a normal lifestyle routine. Solid paycheck, regular work hours, and plenty of time to keep in shape are just some of the benefits during this time. Make sure to do a good job at your duty assignment and you will not have any problems. Additionally, you are technically assigned to the student squadron (Sturon or STUS) and will report there on a regular basis to handle administrative tasks like required training. It is critical to be absolutely on time (ten minutes early is "on time" and on time is late!) for every meeting. Miss a required assembly and you will be placed on the "commander's awareness program" which is a bad way to stand out from your peers. Miss a few more and you stand a decent chance of being thrown out of flight school for lack of military bearing.

During casual status you have the ultimate opportunity to start getting the inside scoop on pilot training, which is like having a cheat sheet for the final exam. During the group assemblies with fellow OAPT students, find the people that have been on station for a few months or are already in UPT and start gathering study materials. Definite items to acquire are *current copies* of the Bold Face/Ops Limits tests and a bootleg copy of the Dash-1. Gather all the intelligence about pilot training that you can, it will make you more prepared for training.

Make doubly sure to keep your nose clean during this time! Frankly, casual status is boring. You came here to be a hotshot pilot and they have you doing routine office work, for crying out loud! Being bored, having a little money, and some freedom now that college is over is a recipe for disaster--if you do not have a positive outlet for you energy. Find positive things to do with your time! I definitely recommend getting your workout routine started and sweating at least six days per week.

Try to avoid the habit of rolling to the big city every weekend to party! This habit will carry over when you enter UPT and it leads to becoming more focused about running to the big town rather than the real reason you came to the base in the first place. Save the big city runs for long weekends and times you have earned a special celebration. Everything you need is either on base or in the small communities nearby. Everything else is just a desire and that can wait. Channel your energy into establishing good workout and study habits and you are a little bit closer to that dream aircraft every single day.

UNACCOMPANIED OFFICER'S QUARTERS - THE UOQ'S

After many years of teaching people to fly, the Air Force has perfected many things about making new pilots and one of the best is the Unaccompanied Officer's Quarters, (UOQs or just the "Qs). Because roughly 300 student pilots are going through pilot training at any given time (along with anywhere from 50-150 in casual status), it is very simple and cost effective to provide housing on base that is geared toward student pilots. The Qs fill that bill perfectly.

UOQs are single, small efficiency apartments that cover all your needs while you are in pilot training. Each comes fully furnished, with a small kitchenette and private bath. Think of it as a step above your college dorm room.

The best part of UOQ is the key to all housing--location, location, and location. They are located a short walking distance from the academic classrooms, simulator building, and the flightline. You can literally walk out your door and be in a classroom in three minutes. How powerful is that? Just imagine having a 30-minute break between training events during pilot training and walking to your room to eat a decent meal? How valuable would it be to your UPT performance to be released from the first schedule of flying during the day (basically a two-hour downtime), going back to your room and grabbing a nap--especially when you are feeling run down? Living in the Qs literally means saving hours of time because you do not have to commute to and from an off-base place. Those hours are money in the bank to your study plan. Imagine if you used those extra hours to chairfly, how better prepared are you compared to the off-base students?

Best of all, there are no bills to worry about paying. Power, heat, and air are all provided; all you need to pay out of pocket for is Internet and cable. What could be easier than that? Each building has free washer, dryer and most have shelters with gas grills provided. Additionally, with a little practice and some proper gear, you can easily clean up a Q room from top to bottom in under an hour, tops.

There is plenty of parking, easy access to the free gym, swimming pool, and you can easily stumble home after a long night at the club. My favorite advantage, aside from the walking distance to work, is the security of living on base. You basically live in a gated community with 24/7-armed security. I have never felt unsafe on a base and with the added benefit of being able to walk into any building and get help ASAP, it's a win-win scenario.

The benefits of living in UOQ far outweigh the negatives, especially since you are here to win your wings, not try to live the hip bachelor/bachelorette lifestyle.

Some of your classmates will get together and get an apartment off base and money savings will be mentioned as a factor. I'm not going to get too far into the weeds in that discussion, but let me make one point. You are here to earn your pilot wings--how many dollars is that worth to you? Is living in an off-base apartment with your buds to save a few bucks worth the commute time (and the cost of study time)? Wear and tear on your vehicle, furnishing an apartment, and the distraction of living downtown are all reasons I would skip it and live on base. If the downtown apartment crew is really being honest, they just want to live a cool lifestyle and use the money excuse as a fig leaf to justify the action. This is the perfect opportunity to set yourself apart and live a lifestyle that reflects your commitment to excellence in life and career.

If nothing else, plan on living in the Qs while you are awaiting pilot training, Phase I and Phase II. Once you get a grasp of what is required to complete flight school, then you can make an informed decision about where to live.

If you are married, for all the same reasons, do everything possible to live in on-base housing. Availability of housing varies from base to base, but again, the benefits to time and focus far, far outweigh the inconveniences of living anywhere else.

RELATIONSHIPS

I know I sound like a broken record but the question remains--why are you here? To earn your wings and become a member of the world's premier flying organization, the United States Air Force. Another tripwire to making your dream come true is in the personal relationship arena.

Girlfriends/Boyfriends--A girlfriend/boyfriend can be the key to why you became a distinguished graduate in your UPT class or, just as easily, a major reason why you washed out. Somewhere in between those two extremes lies the truth about having a GF/BF while you are in flight school.

A good relationship can be incredibly helpful while you are in training. Looking forward to conjugal visits, a sympathetic ear when you bust a ride, and someone to take care of you during visits are all fantastic reasons. On the flip side, a bad relationship can make your life a living hell. Spending hours on the phone reassuring a needy GF/BF, "helping" a significant other plan a future wedding, and on-again, off-again relationship drama robs you of critical study time and takes your mind off of the business of flying. Bottom line, a good relationship is worth its weight in gold, a bad one is just plain toxic to your dream.

Spouses--Just like GF/BF's, a supportive and understanding spouse is a wonderful asset to have in UPT. The added benefit is that you have someone there to cover all your domestic chores on a daily basis and that will give you the priceless gift of additional study time. Clothes washing, shopping, and cleaning literally gives you hours of additional study time that your single classmates do not have. A corollary benefit is that some of your classmates can benefit from your personal situation too. In my study group, a couple of the guys were married and it was wonderful to go to their houses in the evenings to study. Hot food was always put on the table during our chairflying sessions, which was a Godsend for all of us.

Also, a helpful spouse makes a pretty good study partner. I have been amazed how quickly these significant others learn the basics of aviation just by assisting in the study of their student spouses. It is equally invaluable to have someone to shoot study questions at you on a constant basis. Lastly, having a good listener to talk to is invaluable to releasing your own stress in UPT--enough said.

There is a upshot to all this effort on their part and something that bears repeating to them often--the better they support and help you, the better you will do in UPT and the better your assignment will be. Is the chance of earning a F-22 slot to Alaska or the C-130 to England worth their help?

In either type of relationship, married or a girlfriend/boyfriend, you owe your significant other an honest and direct discussion about the realities of Undergraduate Pilot Training. The areas must include the following:

- The time commitment is crazy. The typical UPT day is all of 12 hours, every day. Rarely will there ever be a lunch break--you eat when you can, so there is little to no chance of going home for lunch.

- For all the hours at work, expect a minimum of three to six more hours at night to study. You simply will not have time to do 50% of the domestic duties and be successful in pilot training. Also, kids and chairflying are not in the same universe. Parenting has to take a backseat to your goal--or you could always just quit and give the pilot slot to someone who wants it more.

- The stress level in UPT is high and relentless--your significant other has to understand this today! Even the most relaxed person is going to feel the increased stress level and get snappish, testy, and short tempered with the people they love. The people you care about have to know this is coming, recognize it for what it is, and let it roll off their backs. It is just a fact of life in UPT.

- You do not have the time or focus to mentally work on anything else during pilot training. Learning to fly takes 99% of your focus and brainpower, the remaining one percent is left for the rest of your existence. You have no room for planning weddings, children, vacations, future homes, startup companies, starting a business, running the family farm or any one of the hundreds of crazy distractions I have witnessed students attempt to manage. Go back to your goal and that simple question you already answered, *why are you here?*

If you explain all this to your significant other and they balk at the requirement, do yourself a favor and re-evaluate if you can realistically complete UPT.

If you are married, you need to make an honest assessment if pilot training and the flying career are compatible with your married life. For the single pilot candidate, if this lifestyle won't mesh with your relationship, save yourself a world of trouble and ditch the relationship. The opportunity for pilot training is a once-in-a-lifetime chance and throwing that all away on a GF or BF relationship that probably won't last is a foolish mistake.

The Single Life--Let me assure you, telling someone at a bar that you are a pilot is an amazing pick-up line. After flight school, you will literally have *decades* ahead to use that angle of attack, if you choose, and I recommend you do that *after* you graduate. Here is a nickel's worth of free advice: if you arrive at flight school single, just plan to stay that way until after you graduate. I know, you may be walking past the love of your life, but you should be focused on your goal, not trying to navigate a relationship. Do yourself and your future self a huge favor and avoid any romantic entanglements while you are in pilot training. It is only a year of your life, can you keep your libido under control for that amount time? Remember, the course and direction of the rest of your life depends on your performance over the next 52 weeks.

Please note here, I am only speaking to relationships. What you do on your free time with bars, Tinder, or whatever is completely up to you. My only advice is to be an adult and avoid drama like the plague.

Additional advice, do not get married just before, during, or immediately after flight school. Before or during flight school should be self-explanatory after reading this chapter. Planning a wedding for immediately after flight school (I have seen a wedding conducted on the Saturday following the Friday graduation!) is a bad idea. What happens if you are having problems in the program, wash back to another class, and won't graduate on time? Worse, what if the weekend you plan to get married is now the weekend prior to your 89 checkride (fail it and you are washed out of pilot training checkride!)? Save yourself some time and drama by planning any weddings for a couple of months after UPT, if for no other reason that you will enjoy it more.

Full disclosure--I eloped with my wife in the week between completing the T-37 - Phase II and starting the T-38 Phase. It worked well for me and my wife was a fantastic help to me getting through flight school. So, do as I say, not as I do!

One final warning--do not, under any circumstances, get romantically involved with any of the following: enlisted members or spouses of any military members. Just like a DUI, getting mixed up with either of those two groups will get you kicked out of UPT and the military. I have personally witnessed a student pilot get caught having a consensual, sexual relationship with an enlisted airmen. Two weeks prior to graduation all the secrets were exposed and a world of shit came down on him. Despite being only five rides away from completing flight school and a great follow-on assignment to the airplane of his dreams, he was removed from training, convicted of having an inappropriate relationship and conduct unbecoming an officer, and tossed out of the Air Force. Big Air Force has zero sense of humor when it comes to those relationships, so please heed my warning.

Uniforms

About two weeks prior to attending Initial Flight Training in Pueblo, Colorado, you will be issued your flight uniforms. Namely, you will receive the flight suits, boots, and gloves for flight operations. Use the following guidance to make sure you are ready to go on zero day at IFT or pilot training.

FLIGHT SUITS

As a professional Air Force pilot, you will be spending the vast majority of your working life in flight suits. They are a symbol of your profession and you spend most of the working day, plus many hours away from the squadron, wearing them. Putting on "the bag" will become as easy and comfortable as putting on your favorite pair of jeans and t-shirt is right now. Sounds great, but the first time you slip into one, it is anything but comfortable. They are stiff, uncomfortable, and the new seams have an amazing ability to scrape skin off your neck in minutes. Like all new clothing, when you get your flight suit you need to take some time to break it in properly.

Flight suits is made out of Nomex material, which is fire resistant. Note that I said fire resistant, *not fireproof!* The Nomex in the flight suit will protect you for *a few seconds of exposure to flames during an accident.* It is designed to protect you from a flash fire, not a full flame. After that initial burst, the heat from the fire transfers to the cloths and skin underneath the flight suit. Wearing silk underwear (which melts to the skin in extreme heat) can be a huge mistake in an emergency--something to consider, as you get dressed before work. I make a big deal of this because there is always some confusion about fire resistant versus fireproof. Time and again, I have heard of people sitting around a campfire (especially downrange) and getting badly burned because they used their flight gloves to throw wood on the fire. They stick their gloved hand in the fire and are shocked when they are burned, while wearing *fire resistant* clothing.

On a side note, your flight suit is a poor fabric to wear in normal life. It is hot in the summer and cold in the winner, important to know when you are preparing for a sortie. As the old saying goes, "dress to egress," which means to dress so that if you eject, you will not die of exposure before rescue help arrives.

First, when you go to get your clothing issued, take the extra time to ensure you have the right size. Don't trust the label! Remember, all your gear is made by the lowest bidder to the government contract, so try everything on. Next, take the flight suits to the alterations place and get the Velcro blocks (for the required patches) and your rank sewn on. The student squadron flight commander (who is your "boss" while you are on casual status) will help you with where to go and who to see in order to get this accomplished. While you are there, ask the alterations people to remove the flap of fabric that covers the pen pocket on the left arm. If you forget or if they won't do it, cut this off yourself. I have never seen anyone keep these flaps in place, much less use them.

Finally, take them home and wash the shit out of them. Don't use fabric softener or bleach! Do not wring them out and keep the wash temperature below 180 degrees. They say you can iron and press your flight suits. Don't do that! Only a class "A" moron would iron their flight suits. I toss in a towel with them and wash the flight suits four times in a row as a minimum. After the last round, *wear them!* Put them on as you are puttering around your room and you will be all set for the flight line.

UNDERSHIRTS

While we are on the subject of flight uniforms, let's talk about t-shirts. The official Air Force color now is "sand". This changes regularly and I have seen the regulations change from dark brown, black, green, back to brown and now to sand. This kind of silliness is what it is and general officers like to make changes and leave their "mark" on the organization. I recommend getting between seven and ten t-shirts. I always get the best quality, 100% cotton shirts I can find. Keep most at your home but throw a couple of clean ones in your locker at the flying squadron. Having a good, clean T-shirt waiting for you can feel wonderful after sweating your ass off in the first flight of the day. Also, keep a spare flight cap in your locker as well, one day either you or one of your classmates will need it and you will be a hero for having one handy. Pretty simple stuff, really, but a little effort now will pay dividends in the future.

FLIGHT GLOVES

Gloves are easy. Put the gloves on and wash with soap and water. The motion is the same as washing your hands. When they are clean, rinse and take them off. Squeeze but do not wring the gloves out. Lay the gloves out on a towel and roll the towel up. Once they are dry, you are good to go.

BOOTS

As a military pilot, you fly in boots. Make sure you are issued a pair that fits you properly. Bring a pair of regulation socks with you and *try them on!* It sounds obvious, but there will be guys in your class that just grab the box and walk out. Don't do it, you are becoming a professional aviator and you will spend literally 60-80 hours per week in those boots and to have a bad fitting pair is worse that torture, it is hell on Earth. Get your pair and try them on with the proper socks. Do this right the first time, a little extra time will pay off in the long run, trust me on this one.

Once you have a proper fitting pair, it is time to break them in--*now, TODAY!* Again, guys will wait until the night before the start of training to begin breaking them in. By lunch time the next day, you will see them hobbling around as the blisters on their feet burst and start to bleed. Don't be that guy!

Everybody has their own secret for breaking in boots. Google or YouTube "breaking in military boots" and you will see plenty of detailed instructions. My technique is to soak a thick pair of socks in warm water, put them on my feet, put the boots on, and walk around. The idea is to "walk them dry" as my grandfather would say, that is wear them until the leather dries out. After about a half hour, switch to a dry pair of thick socks and keep the boots on your feet. Today's flight boots are made with modern materials but there is still leather in the construction. Now that suede is the predominate material, you will not need to worry about polishing your flight boots, however, clean boots are still important--especially on checkride day. A quick once over with a small wire brush and you are good to go. Or a very little soap and water followed by the wire brush if you have a really stubborn stain.

A quick word about buying your own boots from the open market: the primary goal of this entire endeavor is to make you a professional aviator. I am a huge believer in making sure you have the very best professional gear and sometimes the government issued personal equipment is not the best. Getting your own boots makes perfect sense, but just make sure if you get boots from the open market that they are USAF flight approved. Take a picture of the regulation allowing your particular boot choice and keep it in your phone. That way if an instructor asks, you have the supporting information at your fingertips. Just so you know, sometimes being different in the military aviation community, especially as a student, irritates instructors and leadership. It is a fine line between being a colorful character and a smart ass. Smart asses tend not to do well in the Air Force. Get the best equipment that works for you, but be prepared to show the documentation that it is legal to fly with it.

I know this sounds like a lot of effort and time for something as simple as issued military boots, but look at it from the Air Force's point of view. You are in training to be in complete control of multi-million dollar aircraft with very little adult supervision. As a commander, can I trust you with this amount of power if you can't manage your own appearance? If you can't do the little things right when you are under the microscope of UPT, how can I expect you to manage the big tasks later on? Ultimately, keeping a good appearance will give the instructors one less item to harass you about.

INITIAL FLIGHT TRAINING

Scheduled length = ~ 30 days
Programed flight hours = 18
Academic tests = 1
Checkrides = 1
Milestones = Dollar Ride, Solo out, 1st Air Force Checkride

While on casual status and just prior to the beginning of Undergraduate Pilot Training, you will be sent to Pueblo, Colorado to attend the Initial Flight Training program. (ROTC students may be sent to IFT in the summer between their sophomore and junior year in college.) Run by Doss Aviation (with direct Air Force oversight), this program simulates Undergraduate Pilot Training and prepares the pilot candidate for the structure and pace of UPT. This program is set up to answer one burning question--can the pilot candidate learn to fly to a specific standard in a designated timeline? Initial flight training has been in place (in various forms) for decades and is structured so that the pilot candidate experiences a snapshot of the speed and stress level of flight school. Additionally, the Air Force gets a look to see if the candidate can learn at the grinding pace of UPT. This is a one-time opportunity school. If you wash out of IFT, you do not have any more chances to complete the program and you will not go to Undergraduate Pilot Training.

Unless a pilot candidate already possesses a Federal Aviation Administration private pilot's license, then s/he must successfully complete IFT prior to attending pilot training. Additionally, when you arrive at IFT, you will be given an Air Force fitness assessment. If you fail the PT test, you will not start Initial Flight Training.

Spanning approximately 30 days and 18 planned flight hours, initial flight training introduces the student pilot to the methodology of Air Force aviation. Stand Up, Bold Face/Ops Limits, and Academic exams are all on the curriculum. All these training elements are explained in detail later in this book. Reviewing these sections will prepare you for what will take place at IFT. Since IFT is built on the Air Force pilot training model, many of the elements you see in Pueblo will be repeated at flight school.

The DA-20 Diamond aircraft is a single engine, 125 horsepower, two-seat aircraft that is well suited for basic flight instruction. The Diamond has excellent flying characteristics and power response in all phases of flight.

Expect to have roughly 25 students in your IFT class. Additionally, there will be other flights in flight training at the same time, consisting

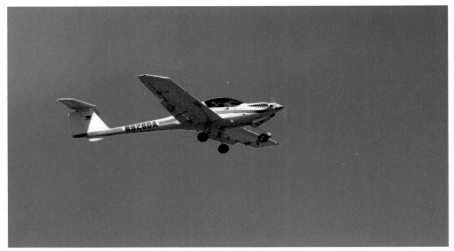

(U.S. Air Force photo/Tech. Sgt. Cecilio Ricardo)

of Combat System Officer (CSO) students and Remotely Piloted Aircraft (RPA) students.

- Day zero--You will inprocess at the Doss facility. Fitness Assessment on this day. Make sure to read the inprocessing guide and follow the instructions to the letter.

- Day one--Expect this to start five solid days of academic instruction and physical training.

- Academic test--50 questions--standard Air Force 85% to pass.

- You are expected to know the DA--20 Boldface and Operating Limits from day one.

All Air Force flight training is broken down into training blocks that have specific objectives that must be met before going on to the next phase of instruction. You will see this method of block instruction for the rest of your aviation career.

Flight block:

101--Dollar ride (see the section on dollar rides)

200--Three flights

300--Six flights. Flight 306 is a "must pass" ride. If you fail this sortie, you go to a progress check (88 ride) with an Air Force instructor pilot
500--Two flights. Pre-solo and solo rides
601--One flight. Pre-check, a practice checkride
790--Checkride

The checkride is like any flight you have made in the 300 block of instruction, except the check pilot does not say anything. Do not let the silence throw you off! All you need to do during this ride is perform the maneuvers to a "fair" level. This means that you are safe and do not require the check pilot's intervention.
Make no mistake, while Initial Flight Training gives you a glimpse of pilot training, UPT is multiple times harder and faster. While IFT can be stressful, it is an excellent opportunity for you to set good habit patterns and expectations for the road ahead. Memorize the Boldface/Ops Limits for the DA-20, arrive at IFT as instructed to the letter, and attack the program--you will do just fine.

DUI--DRINKING AND DRIVING

This is an easy one, but I will make the point because it is important. Almost everyone that arrives at UPT shows up as a Second Lieutenant, which means the Air Force has not invested a tremendous amount of resources in you. Therefore, if you get picked up for drinking and driving, Uncle Sam is not out of a lot of money if you are thrown out. Let me assure you, if you get a DUI while you are awaiting pilot training, while in UPT, or following pilot training, you will be thrown out on your ass. Read that again because it is that important. The only wiggle room you may possibly have is if you hire a high-priced civilian lawyer that can work magic and get the entire case dismissed. What would that service cost you?

Let me give you an example of the stupidity I have seen. Young lieutenant is at a party off base and has had a few drinks. He already gave up his keys because he was going to stay at the party house overnight.

Lieutenant is chatting up a hot, young local girl and she says how much she loves riding motorcycles. Lieutenant is trying to impress her so gets a key to the host's super cool motorcycle parked right outside and he and hottie jump on. They ride down the street 100 yards and the lieutenant turns around and goes straight back to the party house. Local cop see the illegal U-turn and pulls them over. DUI, out of flight school, thousands spent on civilian lawyer—unsuccessfully--and now the man is an ex-Lieutenant. Career over, dream dead and years of effort gone to waste--was it worth it?

I know what you are going to say about the Air Force and the culture of drinking and the Officer's Club. You have a point but everything in moderation, and if you even look at a glass of alcohol, do not drive. An added benefit of living on base is the ability to just walk home.

DRUGS--POPPING POSITIVE

A key factor to remember during every phase of pilot training--concentrate only on today. Everything is "Only about right now". You have started on a long road, do not look too far ahead. Focus on what you are doing today, tomorrow and this week--ignore the road ahead. Dreaming on becoming an F-15E pilot is a waste of time if you don't pass initial flight training.

This is so obvious that I hesitate to even write this section, but enough idiots have completely destroyed their lives, health, and careers so effectively, I will take the time to speak plainly.

Make no doubt, if you ever test positive for an illegal substance, you will be out of aviation, forever. I have never heard of a person popping positive on a drug test and ever flying again. Do you really want to take that chance?

The United States Air Force utilizes the commander's Demand Reduction Program to eliminate drug use in the force. Basically, it is a randomly assigned, no-notice drug test. No matter your rank, age, position, or career field, you can and will be tagged to give a urine sample. Random is not just a catch phase either. I have taken a pee test and had to give another 48 hours later. I asked about it and the tech said that my name just came up again--it is *that* random.

I know the military is a reflection of the society at large, but this is where there has to be a clear distinction. We handle incredibly expensive equipment in hazardous conditions. Also, the amount of killing power placed into our hands is staggering and there is simply no room for someone with an altered mind. I know the country is developing a different morality when it comes to marijuana, but in the military, it is still forbidden. When a positive drug result hits a commander's desk, the paperwork to prosecute and discharge the offender is started within hours.

While I was a T-38 instructor pilot, a fellow instructor popped positive for cocaine. In the investigation, the guy admitted to a one-time use at a party downtown. He was found guilty at the courts martial and got one year in the prison at Fort Leavenworth! A few of his friends went to visit him in prison and during the visit they asked him what it really like in the slammer. "Oh it is not too bad," he answered, "I live in a kind of giant gymnasium that has rows of cots. But what really freaked me out was on my first night in jail, I am laying on my cot, trying to sleep. I hear a strange noise and look over. In the next cot (two feet away), two guys in their fifties are having sex. I covered my head with the blanket and prayed for daylight." Enough said on that topic, right?

All that seems well and good, and you are too smart to get involved in drugs, but there are still things you need to be on the watch for.

Supplements--The body building supplement market is like the Wild West. Any moron with a sink can throw together ingredients and market their own supplement. Military people like to get buff and we are bad about taking something from a store-bought container. *If it comes from this bottle I bought at the store, it must be safe and legal*--sort of like if they put something on the Internet, it must be true. The truth is, you have no idea what goes into the supplements and you are putting them in your body. This happened to a guy I know, he took supplements while hitting a big weightlifting program and popped positive for several types of illegal drugs. When they looked into what he was taking the reason for the positive became clear. Certain ingredients in the supplement were the precursors for synthetic drugs. His life became a living hell overnight! After 9 months and $15K+ of civilian lawyer's fees, he finally cleared his name. What a silly reason to put your career in jeopardy.

Over the counter, overseas--This one caused my blood to run cold because I could have easily made the same mistake. Seems there was a pilot on vacation in Canada. He had a headache, so he went to a local drug store (a chain drugstore that we have in the USA) and bought Tylenol. Headache is cured and he thinks nothing about it. On returning to the U.S., he gets called for a drug test and pops positive for codeine. On popping positive, you are asked to provide proof of a prescription for the drug that is identified. There was no doctor's note and the pilot was screwed. During the research, it was discovered that the Tylenol was the problem. Canadian law allows a small amount of codeine in their headache medication. An honest mistake that took months to clear up. Fortunately, he saved his career, by the skin of his teeth. Be careful out there!!

HAVE A CARE ABOUT WHAT YOU ADMIT TO THE FLIGHT DOCTOR

Before I start this conversation, let me first say how much I admire and appreciate the flight surgeons and medical professionals that do incredible work to keep pilots performing their mission, every day. The entire AF medical system works tirelessly to keep the mission moving and is a key component in our dominance as the finest Air Force in the world.

Having said that, you need to have some care in what you tell the flight surgeon and what is put on medical forms.

A story may give you the best example of what I mean. I know a student pilot, Tim, who was a sharp student and the picture of what you want to see graduate from UPT. Hard working and a great attitude, this guy is an awesome classmate. There is only one problem, Tim is still awesome in every way but did not graduate from UPT.

A couple months before graduation, Tim was on a roll. Ranked very high in his class, he was breezing through the T-1 program and within just a few days of assignment night. He was looking for a C-17 or AC-130 assignment and all the signs looked good for that to happen. Tim woke up one typical morning with a really sharp headache and went to the flight surgeon's morning sick call. After going in, the headache got worse and he started barfing because the pain was so bad. The flight docs called the ambulance to take Tim downtown to the hospital because the base clinic had no real treatment capability. The ambulance arrives and takes him to the local hospital where the civilian doctors saw him. The headache passed, with the help of some medication. The written record for Tim's examination by the civilian doctor included the phrase that the sharp headache is "like a migraine." Little did Tim know it, but those few words dropped a nuclear bomb on his Air Force flying career.

Migraine headaches are strictly forbidden for Air Force pilots, no exceptions and just that quickly, Tim's Air Force flying career came to an end. Once the word "migraine" came back to the base, Tim was pulled out of training. He then went through multiple tests to try and determine what happened during his headache episode. These tests culminated in a MRI on his head. Mind you, all these tests came back clear, no problems at all and the original civilian doctor told the military that he merely put the word migraine on the chart because it could be a possibility, not because it was a fact. In the end, higher headquarters decided to deny all Tim's appeals, waiver requests and he was disqualified from flying. No evidence of a problem, no questionable tests results, no repeat symptoms and a simple statement by a civilian doctor permanently ended a true stud's pilot career before it really started.

So why do I tell you this terrible story? Because you need to have some thought about your interaction with the medical community. Let me say clearly, I am not telling you to be dishonest or not forthcoming in providing information to your flight doctor. But the flight surgeon holds your career in their hands and it is important to be vigilant about the information you provide.

On the flip side of the coin, I understand the flight surgeon community's fear. As medical professionals, they are charged with ensuring the pilots that strap on the jets daily are physically ready to deal with the forces of modern aviation. Their biggest failure would be a pilot they marked as fit for duty having an incident due to a medical problem that caused a loss of life. That is a heavy burden indeed.

QUITTING

This subject really pisses me off, but it has to be discussed before you enter pilot training. Despite reading this book, despite the years of effort, and despite the shame, you want to quit pilot training. Undergraduate Pilot Training is a unique program in the Air Force in that you can quit and be re-trained into another career field. Of course, you have painted yourself into a corner--you can't just quit the next school you attend. Quitting at the follow on school is called "failure to go" and is punishable under the Uniform Code of Military Justice.

There is no shame in washing out of flight school. Not everyone can learn at the breakneck pace UPT demands. A stumble in training or a few bouts of airsickness and you get behind the power curve. Some people can't keep up the physical and mental demands of preforming at the highest level day after day. That is understandable and honorable. Given enough resources, the Air Force can teach pretty much anyone to fly to the Air Force standard, but there are only so many assets available.

You will hear this again and again--do not quit, make them throw you out! It is a long, drawn-out process to wash out of flight school. Everybody meets with some failures, and once you start down the path of being removed from training, a lot of things can happen that makes UPT go your way. A simple change of instructor could make the light turn on for you or a couple of strong rides shows that you can bounce back from failure.

I have been on commander's review boards (the last look by the wing commander to decide if you get another chance at UPT or if you are washed out) and witnessed the wing commander overrule all his subordinate commanders and reinstate a student pilot. He did this because the student made a logical, passionate appeal to be given one last chance. That man graduated from flight school. If you quit, you are not giving yourself a chance to win, or even giving good luck a chance to strike.

No, what I am talking about is the person that wakes up one day and decides that flying is too hard, too much work, not what I thought it would be, I don't like my instructors, or any of the million reasons people use to justify being a quitter. Please, do all of us a favor, if you might quit, don't even bother coming here.

Having said all this, my biggest contempt is for the T-6 solo out-quitters. If you can imagine, there is a group of people who are the worst of the worst. They clear all the hurdles of getting into flight school (taking a priceless slot from someone else), enter training up until they solo out in the T-6 and quit (occasionally the next day). Anyone who does this is a maggot that deserves the scorn of everyone who ever earned his or her wings. Go back to your Xbox life and start bitching about your Air Force benefits and leave the actual flying to your betters.

GET READY FOR UPT!

Undergraduate pilot training is a long, grinding year with the fear of failure hanging over your head. The best advice I can give you to create the greatest chance of success is to get your personal life in order and eliminate as many distractions as possible. You need to have a long heart-to-heart discussion with your family and make sure everyone is aware and understands the commitment it takes to succeed in the Air Force aviation arena. They have to understand that how you perform in UPT sets the stage for rest of your professional life. Here are some pointers that can help you make the picture clear for your family and ease the burden on yourself. The reason they are listed is because I have seen these issues come up, repeatedly.

- Once you know your training dates, make sure your family

knows that you will not be able to attend anything during that year. Weddings, baptisms, and anniversaries are all off the table unless they fall perfectly on holidays or down periods. Be aware, if your base falls behind the timeline, even holidays and weekends can be training days. I once saw a guy quit UPT because his family gave him shit for being unable to attend his sister's wedding. He kept whining to the student squadron commander about getting extra leave that the commander said, "Sure, you can go but you have to DOR (Drop on Request--aka Quit) flight school," thinking that no one would be that stupid. The guy was that stupid and quit the next day--idiot.

Having said that, if there is a true family emergency you absolutely can get leave and take care of business. What you want to avoid are life events that are purposely planned during your training.

- Spend some quality time to make sure your wife/husband knows what will happen day-to-day during pilot training. Twelve-hour days are the standard. You cannot expect to be available to pick up kids from school or sit for a family meal during the week. Every event is subject to change and flight operations come first. Your spouse has to put your schedule ahead of almost everything and cannot pitch a fit if you do not have time to care for children because you have to study. UPT is a fancy way of saying "one-year kitchen pass" in pilot speak.

- Boyfriend/Girlfriend issues--I will make this one simple. Explain the program and the challenges to your significant other, if they balk or if they start causing drama, get rid of them. If you are dealing with drama in your personal life you are not studying for UPT, it is that simple. You must have your head in the game 100% of the time. Once you have your pilot wings, you will have no problem attracting members of the opposite sex, in fact the opposite is true. As my grandmother always said, "girl (boy) friends are like buses, another one is always coming around the corner."

• Put as much of your personal life on remote control as possible. Automatic bill pay is a perfect example. The less administrative chores you have to worry about on a day-to-day basis, the better.

• Eliminate as many distractions as possible. During pilot training, I unhooked my cable and turned the TV around to face the wall. On the weekends, I would go through the five-minute operation to hook everything back up again so I could watch the TV. It was a small point but I made sure that I didn't just flop in front of the TV and let hours pass when I was tired. Today there are tons of distractions, TV, internet, video games, and cell phones are all just begging to steal time from you. Do as you please but when you are picking up the controller to your Xbox, ask yourself "is this getting me closer or farther away from my dream of being a pilot?"

Despite how it might appear, your time as a casual student will eventually end. All the hard work is about to pay off, but you must utilize the golden time between being commissioned as an Air Force Officer until the start of pilot training to ensure your success.

Now, on to Undergraduate Pilot Training!

THE UNIVERSAL TRUTHS OF PILOT TRAINING

The purpose of this chapter is to go over a number of terms, ideas, helpful hints, and concepts that will be universally applicable during all the phases of flight school. In fact, a lot of these areas will be applicable for your entire flying career. I will explain these items now and you will hear me refer to them over and over as we discuss flight school. For example, the prep work and things to remember for checkrides is comprehensive and applies to every checkride you take in Undergraduate Pilot Training.

I wish I could take credit for the following "Words O' Wisdom" but I can't. Credit for this outstanding list belongs to my friend, Captain Courtney Vidt, one of the finest Instructor Pilots I have ever known. I did the research but I never found the original author. If you want to have some words to get you through UPT, put a copy of this list where you can read them every day.

FLYING "WORDS O' WISDOM"

1. There's no replacement for hard work

2. There are Rules and there are Laws; the Rules are made by men who think they know how to fly your airplane better; the Laws (of Physics) were made by the Great One

3.   Always maintain military discipline

4.   Your instructor is always right, even when s/he is wrong

5.   About checkrides: The only real objective of a checkride is to complete it and get the check pilot out of your airplane.

6.   Busting a ride is okay; but you still better be busting your ass

7.   Don't be afraid of anything or anybody, but respect everything and everybody

8.   The ideal pilot is the perfect blend of discipline and aggressiveness

9.   Keep a 'Book of Knowledge' with you at all times; you can learn a lot in the briefing, debriefing and O'Club bar

10. Show up with no call sign; you will "earn" one

11. While in the air, if you have time to think about: girlfriend/ boyfriend, golf, food, or whiskey, something bad is about to happen

12. Before you arrive, leave your ego somewhere on the interstate

13. No alcohol until Friday night unless you are flying on Saturday, then no alcohol until Saturday night

14. Always admit mistakes and make no excuses

15. Don't apologize for your mistakes, they're unavoidable

16. Know which airplane you want to go fly when you show up on Day 1 of pilot training; don't be shy about it, but don't be arrogant either; if they ask you what you want to fly and your answer is "Whatever the needs of the USAF dictate," you'll be wrong.

17. Build a model of the plane you want to fly and keep it on your desk, just so you are clear on what your objective is

18. Help your bros in your class; don't keep secrets from them, don't undermine them and don't ever do anything socially without at least inviting them

19. Work hard and play hard during your year at pilot training; when in doubt, work harder

20. Do stupid stuff and learn from it, but don't do too stupid of stuff that you can't recover from it

21. If you're not doing something, you're doing something wrong

22. If you ever find yourself just "enjoying the view," you're probably forgetting something important; that being said, don't forget to take a few seconds to enjoy the view on every ride; call it "clearing turns" if needed

23. Take something away from every flight, even if it's just an appreciation for getting back on the ground in one piece

24. Your priorities for pilot training are, in order: getting your wings, family, partying, romance

25. You never get points for scaring anyone else in the jet with you

26. Never argue a grade you received on a ride or any portion of the ride

27. Be the master of your fate; you make your own luck

28. He who demands everything that his aircraft can give him is a pilot; he that demands one item more is a fool

29. Be on time and give a shit, no, be 10 minutes early, to everything!

30. If you can learn how to fly as a Lt and not forget how to fly by the time you're a Lt Col, you will have lived a happy life

31. Remember that the radio is only an electronic suggestion box for the pilot; sometimes the only way to clear up a problem is fix it yourself

32. At the end of the day, the controllers, ops supervisors, maintenance guys, weather guessers, and birds are all trying to kill you and your job is not to let them!

33. 90% of all situation awareness is knowing what's going on

34. If you are lost, go faster; you won't be lost as long

35. There's no crying in flying

36. Unless you're in jail, never fight naked

37. Unless he murdered someone in your family, you must bail a fellow pilot out of jail within 12 hours

38. Bitching about the brand of free beer in your roommate's fridge is forbidden; gripe at will if the temperature is unsuitable

39. The ultimate responsibility of the pilot is to fulfill the dreams of the countless millions of earthbound ancestors who could only stare skyward and wish

40. Jesus made you a pilot… honor him!

This is an outstanding list and if you follow it, you just increased your chances of graduating from pilot training!

Pilot training is a daily meat grinder and a typical day is scheduled like this:

0800--Students show at the flight room and prepare for the morning briefing. The students are responsible for getting the weather and NOTAMs.

0810--Instructor pilots end their morning pre-briefing and go to their desks in the flight room. As the IP approaches, their students stand, salute and report in--*no matter the student's rank!*

0815--Formal briefing begins. The day's weather, NOTAMs, and any operational notes for the flight crews to remember are briefed at this time. The Unit Standardization/Evaluation Monitor (USEM) instructor or his assistant, ASEM (Assistant Standardization/ Evaluation Monitor), gives the Stand Up emergency situation oral quiz (explained in detail later) during this time.

0840--Formal briefing ends and preflight briefing begins for the first set of sorties. If you are not flying on the first line, you will listen as the first line student and instructor pilot brief.

0945--First flight students and IPs go to the operations desk to be assigned an aircraft. Second flight students have study time or may be given an impromptu class on some facet of basic aviation. For example--traffic pattern discussion or real-time practice at making radio calls. Additionally, until every student passes his or her first checkride, each student will complete a Bold Face/Ops Limit test every day. *If the class is required to complete a Bold Face/Ops Limit test, make sure everyone completes one before leaving for the day. Woe betide the class that allows someone forget to do their BF/OP!*

Occasionally, the students will have a simulator sortie scheduled, rather than an aircraft or both during the day. Simulators are scheduled and prebriefed exactly like an actual aircraft.

1145--First sortie students return and start formal debrief, second sortie students listen to the discussion and prepare for their instructional sorties.

1245--The second flights of students begin prebriefing and the roles of the first and second flights reverse.

1445--Second flights return to the flight room and debriefing begins.

1600--Academic class begins. Sometimes academics will be taught by an instructor or may be computer-aided instruction.

2000--Students are dismissed for the day. Because of crew rest requirements (12 hours!), students are not allowed to hang around the classrooms or return to the flight room.

Remember, this is just a generic day--1 of 365 at Undergraduate Pilot Training and there are a million variations to all these events. Also, because this is a dynamic environment there will be changes to the schedule throughout the day. Get use to the idea that nothing will go as planned and you must be prepared when the unexpected happens. For example; if there is a ground layer of fog in the morning, academics and flying are flip-flopped. You were planning on a couple of extra hours to prepare for your test in the afternoon--too bad for you.

Flexibility is the key to airpower--expect to hear that phase over and over again.

Finally, what do you not see on this schedule? No lunch breaks or free time. Until the class passes certain milestones (typically after the instrument block) no one is allowed to leave the squadron without permission. Even if you are not flying that day, you will stay in the squadron and you could be tapped to perform some additional duty, if needed. This is to ensure everyone has plenty of time and opportunity to study throughout the day--it is called formal release.

WORK DAYS

You have heard it before, but UPT is a huge commitment of time and effort on your part. The hours involved in flight rooms, academic instruction, simulators, and the aircraft is nothing short of staggering. Despite what the frantic pace suggests, the entire program is well organized and there is actually time away from flight school.

By regulation, you are limited to 12-hour duty days and you must be given 12 hours crew rest before your next training event. This means that the minute you walk into your first event of the day, you are on the clock. Twelve hours later, you better be walking out of your last event or there will be Hell to pay. Crew rest is critically important now and for the rest of your Air Force career and an area where you cannot fudge the time, not even one minute. When you are dismissed for the day, pick up your shit and go home, quickly. You don't have to rush, but hanging around BSing with your friends is a waste of time and you are in a gray area concerning when your training day ends. Also, this applies to your next day of activity. Do not arrive at work unless you have the required crew rest. Although your flight commander and the IPs are monitoring your training, mistakes can and do happen and busting crew rest gets everyone in trouble. Don't ever get into a crew rest problem without having screamed from the rooftops to leadership there is a problem.

Aside from the daily work, UPT runs on a five-day per week schedule, meaning you will be off most weekends and federal holidays. The weekends are gold in pilot training and give you time to recharge, get caught up on studying, and complete domestic chores. One note, this schedule depends on your base's timeline of completing student training on time. In a nutshell, if the base is behind on the timeline because of weather or maintenance delays, all students may be ordered to fly on weekends and holidays.

Finally, AETC takes a gentlemanly approach to the Christmas holidays. Expect your base to shut down sometime around the 23d of Dec and not reopen until after the New Year, 3 Jan. Again, this is dependent on the timeline. If the base is behind the timeline, expect to fly over the holidays. Word to the wise, if you must fly on a weekend or holiday--be cheerful. The IPs will already be grumpy enough for everyone. Besides, you are *flying!*

Progressing through the syllabus

Undergraduate Pilot Training is a specifically designed system, so in order to understand the organization it can be helpful to imagine that you are a widget progressing through a giant factory.

The potential gizmo enters on one side of the process as raw material, talent is there but no form or control--*all thrust and no vector,* as we say. As it moves from station to station, various parts and capabilities are added. Once quality control certifies each step, the gizmo moves to the next station. The process repeats itself until the completed product rolls of the assembly line.

In a very basic nutshell, that is how pilot training is organized. It may seem disorganized to the gizmo as it works its way through, but each event in the training syllabus is designed and tested to take you step by step from know-nothing ground pounder to world class aviator in 52 weeks. The process can best be described as crawl-walk-run-ride a bike. Just as a baby cannot be expected to instantly master the details of running, you are not expected to be able to fly right out of the gate. However, you are expected to attack every training event and that requires your best effort. Most importantly, when you are taught a specific task or skill in aviation it is critical to *remember and master that skill so you must only be taught an item a handful of repetitions.* Learning a task and failing to be able to do that same task in the future is called "regression" and it is bad. This is what is meant when someone says that the learning curve in UPT is "steep". The program demands that you learn, retain, and demonstrate your skills on a daily basis.

The holy grail of the training program is the syllabus. In that document, the timing, requirements, and methodology of your training are explained in excruciating detail. Your instructor pilots and the flight commander will be monitoring your progress every single day while you are in Phase II and III to ensure you are trained properly and making the appropriate progress.

For the student, it is not important to dive too deeply into the syllabus. What is important is to understand that each task you are being taught has a specific end result as its goal. For example, in the beginning of Phase

II you are being constantly taught how to properly land the T-6 aircraft. Over dozens of flights and countless briefing, all the elements of approach, flair and touchdown are pounded into your nugget (head). Once you master the task and that is verified by receiving a checkride in that block of instruction, you will no longer receive much instruction in landings. So when you go out on formation sorties toward the end of the T-6 phase, you are expected to be able to land without any drama. This aspect applies to every training phase and every aircraft you will ever fly.

The bottom line is to study and work hard to succeed in every single training event. Learn what you are being taught day by day and don't look too far down the road. You will finish UPT when you finish UPT and not one-day prior.

AIRSICKNESS

When it comes to airsickness, there are only two kinds of pilots, those who have and those will.
--Timeless aviation saying

Nothing is more humbling than puking your guts out in an airplane. You have a picture of yourself in your mind's eye as the heroic aviator, braving the heavens and it seems your body betrays you at the worst possible time. Adding insult to injury, if you are airsick, you will feel only marginally better getting back on the ground. For all the dread and hand wringing with airsickness, very, very few people actually wash out of UPT from it. In fact, I looked over some of the records at a single UPT base and it appears that only one student over a two-year period was eliminated solely due to airsickness. That is one out of roughly 600. Apparently, this poor guy looked at an airplane sitting on the ramp and started puking. The airmen at Aerospace Physiology worked overtime with this guy but just could not get him over the problem. That man can legitimately say that he gave UPT his best shot but his body was just not built to fly. That happens and there is no shame in that result.

Airsickness is not completely understood, however when the body sends conflicting messages regarding orientation to the brain, this often results in sickness. Some people are more sensitive to this effect than others. In aviation, the inner ear and eyes can be major player in the feedback they send to the brain. In a nutshell, your butt is telling your brain one thing, your eyes have a different perception of reality and the inner ear is screaming that they are both wrong. The body reacts by the classic symptoms--cold sweats, dry mouth and nausea. If the body can't overcome this internal conflict, it rewards you by dumping the stomach.

Other factors that can make you susceptible to being sick are: dehydration, fatigue, stress, and poor nutrition. It sounds like an oxymoron but skipping meals before flying is actually the wrong approach. (Stupid Pilot logic--I won't eat so there is nothing in my stomach so I won't have anything to throw up.)

What type of fuel you put in your body really matters. When your body becomes stressed or begins to feel airsick, your stomach begins to produce acid. Stay away from acidic foods or beverages (i.e. coffee, citrus, tomato sauce, etc.) Dairy, fast food and/or greasy food products are heavy and may contribute to an upset stomach. A diet of bland starchy foods is recommended to help absorb the acid produced in the stomach.

Manifestations of anxiety (MOA) is a broad term that basically covers everything from the fear of flying to being so nauseous that you cannot physically operate the aircraft. Either active airsickness or MOA is meticulously documented in the student's gradebook. While airsickness does not count against you at the beginning of training, it does prevent you from completing all your training objectives, which, in turn, hurts your class ranking.

That is the science behind the condition, but the good news is the Air Force has an amazing track record of helping the determined student pilot to overcome airsickness and get their pilot wings.

During your physiology briefing on spatial disorientation, you will learn diaphragmatic breathing is an effective way to counter both anxiety and reduce nausea. Inhale through your nose for 3-5 seconds, and physically exhale through the belly (versus. chest). This creates a mechanical response in the body, stimulating the parasympathetic response and helps calm the body by working against the conflicting signals to the brain.

Honestly, there is just no way to predict if a particular person will have an issue with airsickness, however there are scientifically proven methods that aid in overcoming this physiological response.

If you go up on a sortie and have an airsickness problem, active or passive, there is a specific protocol you will go through:

1. You are first sent to the Flight Surgeon for a physical check to ensure you don't have an underlying illness that is causing the issue.

2. Most often, the Flight Surgeons send you to consultations with both Mental Health and Aerospace Physiology to address the variety of physiological and psychological factors that can contribute to airsickness.

3. If your airsickness persists, you will most likely be referred back to physiology and begin the Aircrew Rotational Training Program, or "spin protocol". Here you are placed in the Barany chair (pictured above) and spin at a specific rate per minute, accomplishing maneuvers that help acclimate your body to aviation.

4. The Physiology staff will review all you nutrition and preflight actions to make sure you are not setting yourself up for failure.

5. The spin protocol repeats until you beat the airsickness.

This aircrew rotational training program is not fun, however it has been used to acclimate aircrew for over 100 years. When your body does not cooperate with your dreams of being a pilot, this is the time when some students' commitment to UPT will falter, making them potentially lose perspective and get eliminated from the program. Having bouts of airsickness is discouraging and interrupts your training progress. There are

(U.S. Air Force photo/Senior Airman Frank Casciotta)

required trips to the flight surgeon and the physiology flight. This is a gut check time and some people will take this off ramp out of UPT. Despite all the success Physiology has in helping students overcome airsickness, some people will only go to the required appointments. This starts a snowball effect where they are chronically behind their classmates and begin to bust rides for "failure to progress." As day follows night, the student pilot who suffers from airsickness starts down the road to elimination or just plain quits. What is infuriating to me is that they failed to use every opportunity and resource to overcome the airsickness.

I personally know of a guy who had bad airsickness anytime he flew but he had an iron will become a pilot. He overcame his airsickness the hard way. For weeks leading up to flight school he went to a playground daily and conducted his own "spin protocol". He would lay on the roundabout, the ride that spins in a tight circle, and do sit-ups until he puked--*and then repeat it again and again!* That is extreme and I don't recommend you going out and doing it yourself, but you can see the level of dedication this guy had.

It is my opinion that some people who are eliminated from training just didn't have the commitment to be the best or were not at flight school for the right reasons and use airsickness as a cover for quitting. Good riddance, someone else wants your wings more than you do. This won't happen to you because you already made the commitment to being in league with the finest pilots on Earth.

There are some etiquette rules with regard to airsickness.

• Always carry two barf bags. There is a giant box of them in Life Support, keep two at all times. Nothing is worse than to fill up one and have more puke dribbling out of your mouth with no place to put it.

• On your first sorties, have a barf bag under your leg, readily accessible. Fumbling with the bag and yakking on the instrument panel because you couldn't get it out in time is a major foul.

• If you start to feel sick, cold sweats, dry mouth, nausea, there is no shame in pulling the bag out and deciding later that you do not need it.

• If you barf, you clean it up, no matter where that happens. Do not tell your crew chief that you barfed and think you can walk to de-brief. You make a mess, you clean it up, no if, ands, or buts. While I am discussing it, never, ever hand your crew chief a used (filled) sick sack. That will cost you a case of the chief's favorite adult beverage.

The bottom line on airsickness is pretty simple. A percentage of student pilots will suffer from airsickness; it is a natural response to the reality of "unnatural flight." Go to the flight surgeon and ensure you are well enough to fly. Then off to Physiology for spin sessions and you will beat the barfs. It is just that simple. Before you know it, you will be calmly munching on a baloney sandwich while your jet is being tossed around like pinball, meanwhile everyone else will be white as a sheet and grabbing puke sacks. This is a moment when you are super cool and beyond the reach of regular travelers.

Bold Face/Ops Limits Tests

Bold Face--A list of action items that are to be completed during an aircraft emergency that must be memorized and accomplished without the use of checklists or aids. The nature of these emergency actions requires perfect recall and being completed in the proper order. Failure to meet these standards could result in death, injury or major aircraft damage.

Ops Limits--The list of operational limits of an aircraft. Normally includes (but not limited to) airspeed, G-force, altitude, and oil/fuel parameters, etc.

Every airplane you will fly for the rest of you career, military or civilian, will have Bold Face and Ops Limits items you will have to know, from memory, instantly. You will be tested on them constantly and filling out a Bold Face/Ops Limit sheet is the first thing you do to begin a checkride. Screw it up and you failed the check before you walked out the door. Bold Face is the name given to the list of action items that must be done, from memory in an emergency. So if there is an engine fire on the ground, you know to pull the throttle to idle first, then pull the Engine Fire Handle. Additionally, Bold Face covers things like Emergency Evacuation so that you perform the proper procedures before getting out of the airplane and running for your life. Important things like--setting the parking brake!

Ops Limits are the operational limits of the airplane. When the air traffic controller gives you a clearance to climb and it is above the limit of the airplane's capability, you do not have time to say "Okay, can you wait a second while I look that up".

Let me say this very clear, one time, so there is no doubt in your mind. THERE IS NO EXCUSE FOR FAILING A BOLD FACE/OPS LIMIT TEST!

It is the ultimate take home test because you know what is on it NOW! Mastering them is super easy;

1.   Make a few sets of flash cards for both the Bold Face and Ops Limits. I always make three sets, one for my flight suit pocket, one for around the house and one set for the bathroom. Go over them constantly, if you have a moment when you don't know what else to study, go over the BF/OL's!

2.   Get a blank copy of the Bold Face/Ops Limits test (there will be thousands laying around the flight room) and take it to a copy store and run off about 100 of them.

3.   Test yourself every time you have a free minute. Not sure what to study, give yourself a BF/OL written quiz.

4.   Finally, once you get comfortable with the test, start making it more difficult. Play music loud, stand at attention while yelling them to your study partner, take the test while talking to someone on the phone, whatever it takes to add distractions. You will be required to give them on demand under the most stressful time in UPT—Stand Up--and you don't want to choke then.

A critical point to remember--when writing the Bold Face items, you MUST write each step out EXACTLY as they are given on the original copy in your publications. That means, if the master sheet is in all capital letters, you write in all capital letters. You must follow punctuation letter perfect or you bust.

Stand Up

Stand Up is the name given to the oral emergency procedure (EP) test given every day to students during pilot training. In short, the lead instructor (usually a member of the Stan/Eval section) stands in front of the class and sets up an emergency scenario. S/he then assigns the scenario to a student. That student must stand up and take the emergency to a proper, logical conclusion. The only things you have to help you are what you would have on hand, in the aircraft--checklists, etc. Screw it up and you will be sitting for the day. Theoretically, this is so you can "study" but actually, this is to embarrass you and kick you in the tail. Aviation is your profession now, why should Uncle Sam entrust you with an aircraft if you can't even explain how to safely recover the jet in an emergency? Stand Up proceeds like this:

Instructor: "Okay class, situation for today. You are flying solo in your T-6. Ground ops, engine start, taxi and takeoff are all normal. You are straight and level at 10,000 feet, heading to the practice areas, when you see the engine fire light illuminate. Lt Jones, you have the aircraft."

Lt Jones rises and stands at attention: "Ma'am, I will maintain aircraft control, analyze the situation, and take the appropriate action. I will maintain aircraft control by maintaining straight and level flight. Ma'am, am I able to do that?"

Instructor: "Yes, you can maintain straight and level flight."

Lt Jones: "I will analyze the situation by confirming that it is indeed the engine fire light that is on. Is that confirmed?"

Instructor: "Confirmed, it is the fire light that is illuminated, Lieutenant"

Lt Jones: "I will then look at my engine instruments, what do I see?"

Instructor: "You see normal engine indications for the power setting, except the oil pressure is zero and engine temperature is in the red zone and rapidly rising."

Lt Jones: "I will then apply the Engine Fire in Flight Bold Face which is..."

You get the idea and you must be prepared to explain in detail how you will take the aircraft all the way to parking in the chocks or what you would do after unstrapping from your harness after an ejection.

The students chosen to accomplish the Stand Up continues until one of three things happen:

1. You go step-by-step and take the emergency to a logical conclusion. I say "logical" because sometimes the scenario will force you to eject (don't forget your parachute procedures) or ground egress from a burning airplane.

2. You screw up the emergency procedure and hear those terrible words, "Lt Jones, remain standing. Lt Smith, you have the aircraft." At this point you get to stand there while another student handles the scenario. You now have the rest of the day to "study" which means sit at your instructor's desk while everyone else goes to fly--humiliation is not a strong enough word. Since most days last 12 hours, you have plenty (too much) of time to think about your screw up.

3. You go through your procedures, about half way through to recovering the airplane and the instructor says, "Okay Lt Jones, that is good right there, go ahead and have a seat. Lt Smith, why don't you pick it up from there..."

The purpose of this entire exercise is to put you under maximum stress and teach you to perform during that stress. Also, the Air Force gets a good snapshot of how you will react under pressure. Stand Up is challenging, humbling, and a pain in the ass. However, it is a tried and true method to get the very best performance out of students. Best of all, I can attest to you that the stress of Stand Up makes the pressure of a real life emergency almost easy. Don't forget, Stand Up is measured and graded, like all things at Undergraduate Pilot Training. If you fail at Stand Up, the grade is recorded and you will be selected more often to determine if you have a weakness--double whammy!

Here are some keys to success in Stand Up.

• Take your time! When your name is called, adrenalin will pour into your system and your blood pressure will spike. You are nervous and when people get nervous, they try to hurry and finish quickly. Fight the urge to go fast even though it is a natural response. I can tell you from real life experience, in an actual aircraft emergency you have plenty of time to do the correct procedure and think! Very few things in aviation must be done in an instant but if you apply the wrong procedure to an emergency, you can quickly turn a mere hazard into a fight for survival--like shutting down the wrong engine during an engine fire. Don't laugh, it has happened. Take your time standing up. Take a deep breath, you should have been doing calming breaths before they called you. Speak clearly and confidently. Don't shuffle around or look at anyone else in your class, they aren't going to help you anyway. If you apply a Bold Face make damn sure you state the steps perfectly. Don't do anything else from memory, you have checklists in your hand, use them!

• Don't play for time. Having sat through a few hundred Stand Ups, it is obvious to your instructors when you are playing for time because you don't know what to do in a particular emergency procedure. Fumbling with checklists, asking unending questions, hemming and hawing are just a few of the techniques they have seen. You don't have to rush, but decide on a plan of action and go with it. You may make a mistake that causes you to "sit" for the day or you may hit upon a logical alternative that safely recovers the plane. Either way it is better to make a choice of action rather than to remain standing because you pissed off the IP by dawdling.

• Usually, only two students will be tagged for Stand Up on any given day. However, I have seen six students in a row busted for failing Stand Up, a day that eventually took ten students (out of fifteen) to complete. That kind of a day drives schedulers bat shit crazy.

- Declare an emergency! You will be amazed at the number of students (and veteran pilots) that are hesitant to declare an emergency. The real life emergency response system is designed and built to help you--use it!

- The only way to get good at Stand Up is to practice. Get your study partners together and have everyone do one or two scenarios per night. Don't skim over it and be sure to take each scenario to a logical conclusion! If you need to reference a checklist, reference it and read it out loud. Do everything to break your partner's concentration during practice. Loud music, air horns, yelling, whatever--the idea is to think on your feet and overcome distractions.

- Practice, practice, practice normal recovery and post ejection procedures. I would estimate 40% of the people who bust Stand Up are the second student called and all they had to do was recover the airplane or explain the post ejection procedures. Yet they blow them, big time. When you practice, go step by step through *everything* involved in the recovery of the airplane until you park it in the chocks--instead of saying the blanket statement *"I will go back to the airport and land."* What would you say to the fire chief if you stop on the runway due to a fire? What will you say to the air traffic controller when they ask you for their "big three" questions--nature of emergency, souls on board and fuel remaining (in time, not amount!)

- Don't daydream when someone else is working the emergency procedure. It sounds obvious but this one bit me in the ass. It was an early morning show (0430) and I had just gotten tagged for Stand Up the morning prior. I was thinking that I was home free because the Stan/Eval instructor normally runs through everyone in the class before hitting you up again. Sure enough, the second student was called and my mind wandered. The IP saw that I was a million miles away, stopped my classmate during the recovery, and gave me the situation. I had no clue where we were in the scenario and I was fucked. After my extra day of "studying," I never let that happen to me again.

Stand Up is a pain in the ass, and I was happy when I no longer had to do it in UPT. But while you are in pilot training, you will be doing Stand Up, so get used to it and attack it. Be good at it and gain confidence from that ability. Practice, practice, practice.

One last note, as with all things in UPT, Stand Up is recorded and tracked. Your success or failure is noted and affects your scoring and class ranking.

CHECKRIDES

Checkrides are the aviation equivalent of exams. The Air Force uses checkrides to validate the student's training, performance in the aircraft, and application of general knowledge. Despite the ominous sounding name, most checkrides are pretty basic sorties and no cause for anxiety. However, I know most of you will ignore my words so let me arm you with some knowledge to make your checkrides go as smoothly as possible.

The key to good checkride performance is proper preparation--it is that simple.

• Every event, (flight, simulator, and test) in training is aimed toward getting you prepared to pass the checkride for that particular block. Nothing is wasted in pilot training, so anything you are trained in has a logical connection to something else--the building block approach.

• Checkrides are very straightforward sorties. Once your instructor pilot passes you off on the flight prior to the check, you will be scheduled to take it right away, usually the next day.

• The night before the check, make sure your flight suit is perfect.

Clean boots (see the section on breaking in flight boots), perfect patches, and no loose strings are all good ideas.

I know reminders about personal appearance seem silly but checkrides put you under a microscope. If the first impression you give the IP is sloppy or unprofessional, it can carry over to the check. Assuming the entire sortie comes down to a 50/50 judgment call on the instructor's part, what impression do you want them to have of you--sloppy or razor sharp?

- Fresh haircut, or, for the ladies, make sure your hair is within regulations--not even close.

- All your publications and checklists are subject to being examined during the checkride! Make sure they are 100% perfect because you will feel like a fool if you bust for pubs.

- You will complete a Bold Face/Ops Limits test at the start of the check--don't screw it up or your day is over without even stepping out the door.

- Generally, the check pilot will give you the ground evaluation at the beginning of the check. This is where your hard work and studying pays off. The harder you have studied and practiced, the shorter this time will be. As a check pilot, I have several questions I like to ask that cover a wide range of knowledge on the aircraft and the operational environment. If I ask you a question and you answer quickly and confidently, so I know you have a solid grasp of the subject--time to move on. I especially won't waste time if I am hearing quotes and phrases from the particular publications involved. However, if you are vague, seem hesitant, or are just plain wrong, then I am going to start digging to see how much you really know and how much is fluff. This is the difference of a ground evaluation being 15 minutes or over an hour. I will take the time to see how much you really know because I am deciding whether or not to bust you.

• The check pilot is not your friend and you are not funny. Certainly, be friendly but not chummy. While you are going over the briefing and ground evaluation, stay 100% focused on the task at hand. No joking or BS--be a professional at all times.

• For the sortie itself, imagine you are taking your dad or a respected college professor for an airplane ride. Explain, very lightly, the things you are doing during each part. Don't treat the check pilot like an idiot! However, if you are totally silent the whole time s/he might wonder, "Does this student know xyz is happening?"

• Do not ask your check pilot operational questions--they will not tell you and you have just opened yourself up to a long line of questions.

• Beware the "idea fairy"--checkrides are an evaluation of your ability to do things you have been trained to accomplish and already know. Therefore, if you find yourself doing something brand new or have a new way of doing something--STOP!

• Finally, it is a certainty that Lt Murphy will be along during your checkride--if something can go wrong, it will happen on your checkride. Just roll with it and keep working to complete the flight. If real life problems keep getting in the way of completing the mission (i.e. radio problems, aircraft malfunctions, whatever) the check pilot will step in.

• Occasionally the check pilot may ask to see you do a maneuver again. There are two possible reasons for this--1) You have done the maneuver marginally and it is borderline if s/he can pass you on it. 2) It is the best the check pilot has ever seen and wants to see if you can do it again. Which is more likely? If you are asked to repeat a maneuver, you are getting a second chance so make sure you nail it.

I have my own story to illustrate this one. I was on my mid-phase checkride as a student in the T-37. On the profile, I flew us up to the auxiliary field and did a touch and go. Sure enough, on the climb out, after the landing, I screwed up and forgot to retract the landing lights. The check pilot took the jet, retracted the landing lights and handed it back to me. Automatic bust! After that, the pressure was off so I just went through the rest of the profile, almost laughing my way through. On the way back to base, the check pilot asked to fly the recovery (return to base) and shoot the first landing, I said "sure" (like I would say no!). Flying to the runway, the check pilot turned directly into another airplane and was told to "breakout"--exit the pattern and start over. As he climbed out after his mistake he turned to me and said, "I guess that takes care of your little landing light problem." I passed the ride! The two take-aways for you? 1) Never give up on the sortie! 2) Relax you will perform better!

- If you make a mistake, even one that is an automatic bust, keep flying the sortie! Don't give up, you do not know what will happen. Complete the profile and maybe something will go your way.

- Once all required items are complete and the check pilot has flown any requirements s/he needs, you may be asked, "Do you want to fly anything extra--it won't count against you?" The answer is NO! There is no benefit to any additional landings or maneuvers. Be very polite, but say NO!

- If you bust, stand tall and take it like a professional. Don't argue, but if you believe an error has been made, state one time what the problem is and see what happens. If the check pilot busts you anyway, politely explain why you disagree and leave--when dismissed. You will not change anyone's mind by arguing or getting emotional. When you are dismissed, go straight to your regular instructor pilot and flight commander to explain the disconnect. The flight commander may decide that a mistake or misunderstanding has taken place and there is a process for changing your grade. Think "calm and professional" the whole time.

• Ask around for intelligence on your assigned check pilot! Every pilot has favorite subjects and questions they like to ask. Do your homework and be able to nail the areas your check pilot will ask about or quirks s/he about flying.

Checkrides are just a fact of life in all aviation but especially in the Air Force. Follow these simple ideas and you will do just fine.

WASHING OUT, BY THE NUMBERS

It is an unfortunate fact of pilot training that sometimes good people try very hard but fail to meet the high standards of USAF flight school and are eliminated from training. Given an unlimited supply of flight hours, manpower and resources, pretty much any person could be taught to fly, but the required speed of learning in UPT is just too high to allow for that option. If you can't keep up with the pace, you cannot stay in pilot training.

For this discussion, we will take a look at the washout rates currently seen at the pilot training bases. Keep in mind that the rate fluctuates on a regular basis and occasionally a base may spike up or down in wash out rates for any number of variables.

When I was in college (mid 1980s), Reese AFB was bragging that they were running a 40% wash out rate, the highest in Air Training Command. That number has come down considerably and in my opinion, it is because the quality of students entering flight school is better from the get go and the screening processes is more sound. I refuse to fall into the old man trap of believing that pilot training was harder in the old days and "kids today" are just fat, lazy, and mollycoddled.

There is very little difference in the elimination rates of the main UPT bases--Vance, Columbus, and Laughlin. I looked at the rates and the percentage differences between the three are usually less than 1 or 2%. ENJJPT (Sheppard AFB) has consistently run a lower rate and I think that is because their selection process is more restricted. It is harder to get into ENJJPT to begin with so their washout rate is better.

Pilot training washout rates by base and phase:

	PHASE I	PHASE II	PHASE III
Vance/Columbus/ Laughlin	4%	10%	(T-1) 4%
			(T-38) 2%
Sheppard	0%	4%	2%

These are simply numbers, so what can you take away from all this? You have an excellent chance of completing pilot training once you get there. The Air Force screens out most people who would have not made it through Undergraduate Pilot Training. Most importantly, once you complete Phase II, the T-6 phase, the odds of pinning a set of wings on your chest are on your side!

What causes most people to wash out of flight school?

I literally get this question every few days and here is my personal opinion. Most people wash out of flight school in a three-step process:

1. The candidate gets behind in their training due to a minor reason--airsickness, bust a ride, or an academic test--and they begin to lose confidence because they are not used to failure and graduation seems very far away.

2. That loss of confidence allows airsickness, stress, and self-doubt to creep in to their mind. Once it takes hold, the self-doubt is a cancer.

3.   When the confidence (hope) is gone, they quit, give half-hearted efforts, or subconsciously allow the UPT system to throw them out.

Either way, it is a rare day when I see a student removed from training that worked hard, had a good study crew, and kept a great attitude.

THE UPT GRADING SCALE

All maneuvers are graded and all flights get an overall grade. Some areas are more important than others and can determine the overall grade. Hence, you can fly every maneuver to a "good" level but hook the flight because you made an "unsat" on judgment. (Basically, you were a bonehead about something.)

The grading scale and definitions are:

Unsatisfactory (U)--The student is unsafe, unable, or lacks sufficient knowledge, skill or ability to perform the operation maneuver or task.

Fair (F)--The student performs the operation, maneuver or task safely but has limited proficiency. Deviations occur which detract from performance and/or verbal prompting is required from the instructor.

Good (G)--The student performs the operation, maneuver or task satisfactorily. Deviations occur which are recognized and corrected in a timely manner without any verbal prompting from the instructor.

Excellent (E)--The student performs the operation, maneuver or task with a high degree of skill, efficiency, and effectiveness.

STRESS

Here is a little secret, Undergraduate Pilot Training is stressful. Flight school is designed to be hard and stress is a major factor in increasing the difficulty. This is done on purpose and after 100+ years of aviation, the Air Force is pretty good at it.

An old adage at flight school compares student performance and stress to a violin string. If the string is too loose (no stress) it does not make any noise and does not perform as it was designed. Too tight, you might make some bad music for a while but soon enough the string will break. Fine-tune the string (the stress level) and amazing music is made.

Through decades of training and the crucible of combat, the Air Force has perfected flight school to where the proper amount of stress is placed on you on a daily basis. Through academic tests, Stand Up, and EP quizzes, UPT is meant to get the very best performance from you at all times. Add in flight operations in a brand new aircraft, equipment, and clothing, and you have a recipe for maximum stress. It is critical to raise your level of performance at every milepost because you are being taught the art and science of aviation in flight school; at your next assignment you will use your aviation knowledge to turn an aircraft into a weapon of war.

Chairflying

This will sound like total BS, but no other activity will factor in to your success at pilot training as much as your use and mastery of chairflying.

Despite what Wikipedia and spell check says, chairflying is a real thing and a critical key to your success at UPT. To boil it all down, chairflying is the word we give to active visualization of the actions involved in flying an aircraft. This is a complicated explanation to something that is pretty simple in application. In layman's terms, chairflying is the act of mentally walking yourself through all the elements and activities of a pilot training sortie--soup to nuts and everything in between. The more detailed you can do this visualization, the better you will do when you are actually in the airplane.

This is how it is done--sit down in a chair. No really, do this right now--sit in a chair. Eliminate all distractions, TV off, turn off your computer, IPod, phone, and anything else that is an interruption. Close your eyes and imagine you are in your car, getting ready to drive to the store. How would you go about moving the car from point A to B? Describe it out loud and move your hands like you were actually doing it. Close the car door--*your left hand reaches out and pulls the imaginary car door to you.* Adjust the rearview mirror--*right hand reaches up to where the mirror would be.* Start the car--*right hand moves where the ignition switch would be and turns the key.* What are you expecting to happen as you turn the key? *Say out loud what those instruments are reading, point to where they are.* Noises, dashboard lights that illuminate, and engine instruments are just a few things to describe the engine start process. This is chairflying!

Chairflying is critical for your success in UPT because good visualization practice is guaranteed to work. I remember watching Jack Nicklaus being interviewed on why he was so successful at golf when he grew up in Ohio, with its notoriously long and brutal winters. Besides some God-given talent, Jack gave credit to his ability to imagine the shots he wanted to make and then stepping up to the ball to make them. He told the reporter that he spent a tremendous amount of time visualizing the perfect stroke and exactly the kind of swing he needed for every situation. Once you see something in your mind's eye, stepping forward to make it happen almost becomes easy. This can happen in the military arena as well. Prior to going on missions, Colonel Jack Broughton (as described in his book *Going Downtown*) would stand in front of a giant map of the Hanoi area and visualized the bombing mission his F-105's were about to fly. He literally stood over the map and, with his hands, walked step-by-step through the mission--from start to finish.

It is a proven fact, by accurate and methodical chairflying, you will ensure you graduate from UPT and the more detailed you are, the higher you will rank in your class.

Okay, you grasp the concept, so let's put into use. The day you get your in-flight checklists, start chairflying every day. This can be as simple as a few minutes to go over the strap-in procedures, a longer time to walk through the checklist from engine start to line-up check, or a full-blown sortie from beginning to end--which should take about an hour. Once you get the hang of it, you will be chairflying every high-threat event in pilot training. Stand Up, checkrides, and ground evaluations are just a few of the events chairflying will help.

There are a number of ways to make chairflying more effective.

• You will be issued posters of the interior of the T-6 and your follow-on aircraft as part of your academic publications. Hang the poster (we call it a Paper Tiger) on the wall and park your chair directly in front of the poster and go over every checklist. Speed and accuracy in checklists makes your instructor happy, and a happy instructor ensures you get good training.

• Get your classmates involved in your chairflying sessions. If Joe Bag of Doughnuts is going over the start engine checklist and misses a step, both of you just learned a lesson. That is value added for everyone.

• When you get the hang of chairflying, it is time to turn up the distractions. Now is the time to turn on the TV, IPhone, and noises. Throw things like waded up socks at your bud during sessions. Anything to throw off the rhythm of the person in the hot seat. You will be really hitting on all cylinders when you start asking the guy in the seat ground evaluation questions while they are chairflying a full sortie profile from beginning to end.

• Now expand chairflying principles to other aspects of pilot training. Stand Up is the perfect area to chairfly and if you can do it--practice in the flight room with members from your class. Go through all the motions of standing at attention and working EPs out with your buds. Another proven fact is that you perform better in the actual situation if you practice visualization in the physical location you will be tested.

Why is this important, you ask? UPT is an insanely fast learning environment. Drinking from a fire hose is a frequently used and is an accurate metaphor. You do not have enough flight hours in the airplane to go over and over basic elements of flying (like switching radio frequencies or completing checklists in a timely manner). Each sortie has specific training objectives and if you spend all your time fumbling over things you were taught two flights ago, you are getting behind. Remember, getting behind means getting washed out. Time and again in Commander's Review Boards, I hear hard working students beg to be allowed one more chance at flight school. A common theme in their requests to stay is an acknowledgment that they did not do a good job learning how to chairfly and that they will do more and better chairflying if given another chance.

Chairflying is a simple and powerful tool to solidify what you learned each day and prepare you for your next sortie. It works, so do it!

CHECKLIST DISCIPLINE

From the first day you fly an Air Force aircraft to day you retire, you will have the phrase "checklist discipline" pounded into your brain. Checklists are a time-tested cornerstone of military aviation, and if you cannot or will not use them, you will be eliminated--it is as simple as that.

Checklist discipline is the ability to accurately determine which particular procedure is needed at the correct time during a flight and properly follow the listed steps to a logical/safe conclusion. Interesting words, but what does it mean on practical level? It means that for every action in aviation, there are procedures how to conduct the flight from beginning to end. To help you remember the proper order and the sequence of those procedures, a summary (checklist) is printed for the pilot to use. Most are simple and follow common sense--i.e. Before Starting Engine Checklist, Starting Engine Checklist, etc.

Where it gets critical is when an emergency occurs. There are certain actions that must be executed from memory (Bold Face) but then you *must* select the right follow-on checklist and execute the steps.

Student pilots generally make the following mistakes:

- Not using or trying to complete a checklist from memory

- Not finishing checklists

- Skipping or missing items on the checklist

- Using the wrong checklist for a given situation

- Starting, then stopping a checklist to use a different checklist

- Starting a checklist, then becoming distracting and not finishing a checklist

Here are a few rules of thumb to remember about checklists:

- While chairflying, use your checklists and *know* each step you accomplished--don't just give lip service to the steps.

- Remember this: checklists are like gates on a farm, if you open one, you must close (complete) it. Failure to complete a checklist is an automatic bust and the reason many good pilots have crashed airplanes in the past. There is a reason the Air Force hammers this point--it is written in blood!

- You have to be able to halt a checklist and go back to it without becoming confused. It is not unusual to be working a checklist and have to make a radio call or deal with another issue. You must be able to stop, handle the pressing issue, and then return to the checklist. The ability to do this is the hallmark of airmanship.

- I recommend reading over several checklists per day while you are in Phase I & II. Make a simple paper copy of the checklists and go over them while sitting on the toilet. It sounds silly, I know but that is all the time you need to review the checklist during any particular day, otherwise you are wasting time. Understanding the language and acronyms makes you smoother in the jet and hence your IP is happy. Happy instructor pilot equals better, quality training--better training equals SILVER WINGS!

Checklist and the discipline it takes to use them correctly is a basic foundation of Air Force aviation. Getting good habits from the get go is critical for your success in UPT.

EMERGENCY PROCEDURE QUIZZES--EPQ's

In addition to Boldface tests, your class will be given a weekly test on Emergency Procedures (EP) and general knowledge, tailored to your level of training. The specific day of the test will vary, some flights take the EP Quiz every Monday, some every Friday but you will get one every week. As usual, 85% is passing and a failure gets you grounded for the day. EP quizzes are 25 questions in length and can be given electronically, but are usually on paper. Unlike academic tests, this test and the Boldface/Ops limits exam will be given in the flight room.

This test is not especially difficult; study the material you are told to study but pay special attention to all **notes, warnings and cautions** in the Dash-1. AETC loves to pull questions from these areas to ensure you focus on them. Chapter Three is always a favorite (Emergency Procedures), so if you are ever at a loss for what to study--review the **notes, warnings, and cautions** from the EP chapter. This is time well spent for both EP quizzes and Stand Up.

THE DASH--1, NOTES, WARNINGS, AND CAUTIONS

The Dash-1 manual is the Flight Manual that describes the aircraft you are operating. A better way to explain it is to say the Dash-1 is how the *Air Force* wants you to fly the airplane. They own it, so you fly it the way they want it flown, it is as simple as that. Throughout the regulation there are side notations that highlight areas of emphasis, these areas are labeled **notes, warnings, and cautions**. The Air Force defines them as follows:

Note: An operating procedure, technique, etc., which is considered essential to emphasize. *In "pilot speak," it means this is the way the Air Force wants you to do this because we own the airplane--i.e., do it!*

Warning: An operating procedure, technique, etc., which could result in personal injury or loss of life if not carefully followed. *We say that warnings are written in blood because some poor Joe Bags died because of it.*

Caution: An operating procedure, technique, etc., which could result in damage to equipment of not properly followed. *Cautions are written because metal was bent when some idiot did something stupid and big Air Force wanted to make sure you don't do anything that dumb again.*

I highlight these areas because sometimes new students get overwhelmed by the sheer volume of material they are responsible for knowing. If you are at a loss for what to study, delve into the notes, warnings, and cautions. I guarantee you will be tested on the material and especially any numbers associated with them.

Although these subjects may seem disjointed, on the surface it is critical for you to understand and apply all the tips and techniques I've listed for you. Aside from making your transition into UPT easier, you will use some of them, like chairflying, for the rest of your flying career. Refer back to this chapter again and again as you progress through flight school. Now we will take a look at Undergraduate Pilot Training in depth as we break down each phase of training.

This chapter is meant to give you a common frame of reference and a familiarization of terms that you will hear at pilot training. These ideas may seem random and disjointed but they will flow seamlessly once UPT begins in earnest. Enough of the preliminaries, let's go to zero day!

UPT--PHASE I

Before getting into the details of pilot training, let me give you the most important piece of advice you must know before you start UPT.

ATTITUDE IS EVERYTHING! No matter what happens in flight school, you must bounce back from failure and let me assure you, you will fail spectacularly during UPT. Do not let a failure fuck up the next maneuver, pattern, or sortie because you are still stewing on the previous screw-up. Let it roll off your back like a duck. Humble yourself and learn from your classmates. Help goes both ways, so help the person that is struggling in a particular area--they will help you when you hit a rough patch (and you will). Attitude is everything, and it is the one factor that is impossible to teach.

Phase I
Scheduled length = 31 days
Programed flight hours = 0
Academic tests = 3 (Physiology, Life Support, Survival)
Milestones = Zero day, Indoctrination to UPT, Physiology, Parachute Landing Falls, Chamber Ride, 1st Academic test

Congratulations, you have successfully made it to Specialized Joint Undergraduate Pilot Training (SJUPT)! That will be the last time you will hear anyone will call it SJUPT until you hear those words again at graduation, moments before you cross the stage to accept your wings. Everyone calls the school you are about to enter UPT, Undergraduate Pilot

Training, or just flight school. Only the non-flyers call is Specialized or Joint.

Close your eyes for a moment think about that nexus in time--your name is called, your picture comes onto the screen as you walk across the stage to be handed *your* wings. Family comes forward from their seats and snap pictures, as your chest is ready to burst with pride. You tackled everything weather, instructor pilots and fickle aircraft could throw at you and *you conquered them all* and won. Whatever happens for the rest of your life, you walk with pride knowing you succeeded in the U.S. military's most difficult training. That kind of a success marks a person's soul, forever.

Now Undergraduate Pilot Training begins for real! It has been a long road to get to this point, but now all the hard work and preparation is about to pay off. Of course you are excited and ready to hit the flight line today, but this is the Air Force, and we never do anything fun without squeezing the happiness out of it first. Before you start the business of learning how to fly, you have to go through the pain of inprocessing to flight school--even if you have been at the very same base for months. It is rather painful, but it is a perfect lead-in to the rest of your career. The entire journey to your wings begins with Zero Day.

Zero Day--The adventure begins! Zero day is a marathon of briefings and presentations by leadership that sets the tone for your time at flight school. It will be a bit of a letdown but this first day is a long and tedious bore with no flying involved. You will arrive at the student squadron (Sturon or STUS) in your service dress uniform and begin formal in-processing. Be on time and double check that you uniform is perfect.

For the first time, you will meet all your new classmates and it is interesting to see how everyone begins to size each other up. These fellow students will be some of your best friends forever and this is where it all begins. Typically, there are 15-25 students in each class, and that can fluctuate easily between the two extremes. Class size is driven by the base's current student timeline and flight capability.

Do as you please, but my advice is to make a minute-by-minute effort to be on good terms with everybody in your class. I know you will have a blow-hard know-it-all sitting right beside you every day, but bad blood between flightmates ensures poor performance for everyone. You are there to earn your wings, nothing else matters, right? Besides, just vow to be a better pilot than him; that fact will hurt the jerk worse than thumping him anyway.

Leading the show, the Wing Commander briefs you on the expectations of a student pilot and the takeaway from this briefing is to never be called or sent to the Wing CC's office! To go to the Wing Commander's office is to be in trouble or on the last stop before being washed out of the program. Your mantra needs to be "Stay out of the wing king's office" and every action you make going forward should include the thought--could what I am doing get me sent to see the commander? If the answer is "Yes", stop what you are doing!

After the Wing Commander comes a parade of senior officers who each get about an hour to tell you the do's and don'ts of UPT. This is so if you screw up while in flight school and get thrown out, you can't run to your member of congress and cry "No one ever told me…" Don't laugh it happens, even now.

Do yourself a favor, once you finish all the briefings, get your service dress uniform properly dry cleaned, replace all the hardware on it to perfection, and store it under a dry-cleaner's plastic bag (on a quality hanger) in your closet--including your perfectly pressed blue shirt. It will save you a mountain of time and pain a year from now.

The briefings and in-processing procedures take all day to complete. Everything is pretty easy, but just make sure you are in place early for each briefer and that you bring what you are told to each assembly. If your instructions say to bring 10 copies of your orders to each briefing, then do what it takes to get 10 copies of your orders for each briefing! It sounds simple but I assure you, someone will bring two copies (or no orders at all) and the ensuing ass chewing will waste everybody's time. This is time you could be using for something related to becoming an Air Force pilot.

Keep an eye on the schedule! The class schedule is posted online or emailed to you and it will change dramatically daily, sometime hourly, based on a multitude of reasons. Make sure you check the daily schedule *several times throughout the day.* Also, create a new email account and use it only for pilot training. Make sure you have it set up to go straight to your phone. Every day, the flight commander will email the next day's schedule. Additionally, changes to the current schedule will be emailed, and you're expected to catch all changes and be in place, 100% of the time. This is a "no fail" requirement, so don't screw it up!

No one is going to baby you through the program, get used to having your crap squared away.

During Phase I, you must take *and pass* the Air Force Physical Fitness Test. If you fail, you do not report to the flight line. Pass your test!

REPUTATION

One element that truly separates the military from civilian life is reputation. As an Air Force pilot, your reputation (or lack of it) is the single biggest factor in your happiness and success in your profession. Bold words, to be sure but the reality is there every day. If you are known as a team player, someone who puts out every day, works hard to master your aircraft and profession, and is willing to step up and help the squadron, you are worth your weight in gold. Opportunities come to those guys long before the selfish or foolish ever get a chance. Air Force pilots have the stereotype of being cocky, but that attitude is earned. And, as my Dad always says, "It ain't bragging if you've done it."

As important as your reputation is, you would think that people would guard them most closely. I have seen, time and again, pilots destroy their reputations in a moment of bad decision making and their lives turned to crap. We live and work side-by-side with our wingmen every day-- especially downrange. Looking at someone and thinking, "That dude (or dudette) has my back" is the greatest compliment on Earth--the opposite is true, as well.

If I had to put into one sentence why pilots destroy their reputation, it would all revolve around putting themselves above the other person/ class/flight/squadron/wing. Shacking up with spouses (not their own), ducking unpleasant additional duties, and stealing from a classmate are all just symptoms of a thought process that says, "I think I am more important than you, so screw you". Also, if a guy screws you over so he can go home early, what do you think he's going to do when the missiles start flying and people are dying?

Your reputation begins day one at UPT. Be the pilot you want beside you; train hard, know your airplane and profession, and volunteer to help the cause. These are the ways, brick-by-brick, that you will build your reputation. It surely does not come overnight and it does not come easy, but things that matter rarely do.

Keep it Positive

Understand this, UPT is a grind. The pressure is always on, the instructors are relentless, and statements like "just remember, you are only six rides away from being outta here", bombard you. It is easy to get down and get crabby. Everybody has moments of being low, but nobody wants to be around the "negative Nancy" for very long. We all have bad days, and it is virtually a requirement for a good military pilot to complain loudly to God and the world when things suck. That is fine, what I am talking about now is the guy (or gal) that just won't let it go. We all know the situation sucks out loud, but a douchebag has to yammer on and on about it. Don't be that girl or guy! As an Air Force pilot, your reputation starts here, and an overly negative attitude is a bad thing to have attached to your name.

We have an expression in the military, fake it until you make it. What that means is that even if you are feeling pissed off and mad at the world, say something funny and keep the mood light for everyone. Force a smile on your face, even when you don't want to and eventually things will get better. Don't be the grumpy early morning turd that no one wants to sit next to--keep your attitude light and it will lift the entire group. A positive attitude is infectious and helps everyone get over the hard knocks of flight school. They say timing is everything, and a perfectly timed joke at the just the right moment will make you a favorite person amongst your classmates and the instructors as well.

Help the cause

There are tons of small tasks that must be accomplished by the students during your year in Undergraduate Pilot Training. Frankly, most are tedious and boring but they have to be completed, hell or high water. If you want to quickly earn a solid reputation as a good wingman, volunteer for a few of these tasks and do a good job! From my experience, completion of the tasks is where you see the biggest failures. Be a job-closer and you are someone worth being around. Pulling your fair share, plus a little more, makes the class work, enhances your reputation, and avoids the chewing out that will come down like thunder if tasks are left undone. The take away for you is this--help the cause by volunteering.

FLIGHT PUBLICATIONS

Count yourself lucky, keeping your publications up-to-date is vastly simpler today than it was just a few years ago. The technological ability to manage and organize vast amounts of information has finally hit the Air Force and made a dreaded task, easy. On zero day, you finally get your own set of publications or just "pubs" on a CD. Additionally, you may be issued a few publications in hard copy format, but that is more the exception than the rule.

As an FYI, computer thumb drives are absolutely forbidden in Department of Defense (DoD) computers. It is too easy for adversaries to put viruses on the drives and infect the DoD computer system--rumor has it that it has happened in the past! Plugging a thumb drive into any DoD computer trips a warning system and you are busted instantly.

In this packet of goodies you will get life size posters of the T-6 Texan II cockpit panels. Take these posters home and build yourself a Paper Tiger cockpit in your room. The idea is to make a life-size T-6 cockpit in your living room where you can chairfly the habit patterns of flight. Use your imagination, but in the end, you want as close to a life-size cockpit mock up as you can make. On a blank wall, hang the poster of the front cockpit panels. Place a good chair in front of this and a toilet plunger for an aircraft control stick. Two tall boxes go on the left and right sides to hold the side panels and you are ready to chairfly! More on chairflying later.

G-SUIT, MASK AND HELMET FITTING

During Phase I, your class will get fitted with your G-suit, harness, oxygen mask, and flight helmet. This is a simple operation and there are just a few high points to remember.

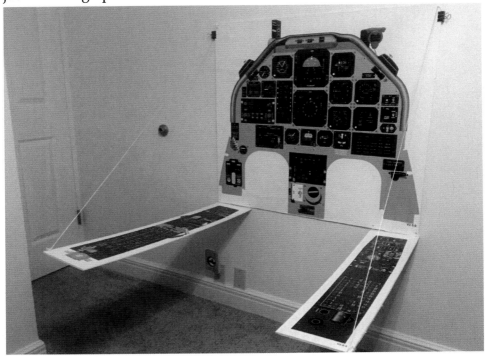

Schedule your own appointment for the fittings at Aircrew Flight Equipment (AFE) and allow at least 45 minutes for the G-suit and harness. Also, allow another 30 minutes for the flight helmet and oxygen mask. This will give you plenty of time to get it done. It is a critical to get the proper fitting the first time on this equipment because ill-fitting flight gear is literally torture—no-shit torture.

While we are on the subject, take care of your flight gear. Some pilots are pigs and don't clean their O2 mask properly, leave trash in their helmet bag, and are just plain slobs. My philosophy has been pretty simple, take good care of your gear, because when you need it to work properly, your life is in the balance. A little daily TLC will keep it working like a champ when the chips are down.

BLINDFOLD COCKPIT CHECK

Because the T-6 is a tandem-seated aircraft and the instructor pilot cannot reach over your shoulder and reach the controls, you will need to be able to safely locate several cockpit switches prior to your first flight. This is done during a no-kidding, blindfold cockpit check. You are blindfolded and sit in the simulator or actual aircraft. The instructor calls out items from the list below and you must put your finger on that item of control.

- Emergency Firewall Shutoff Handle

- Canopy Fracturing System Handle

- PCL Cutoff Finger Lift

- Flap Selector

- Landing Gear Handle

- Emergency Landing Gear Handle

- Defog Switch

- Back-up UHF Radio

- Bus Tie Switch

- PMU Switch

- Prop Sys Circuit Breaker

- Pressurization/Ram Dump Switch

The blindfold cockpit check is as old as aviation itself and a perfect test to show how effective chairflying in your Paper Tiger can be. Set up the life-size posters of the cockpit and practice!

Aerospace Physiology

It is a fact that aerospace physiology training is just plain fun. There is little threat (we will cover that later), the training is interesting and you will apply what you learn throughout your professional aviation life.

In a nutshell, aerospace physiology is the science of how the aviation environment affects the human body. In the 110+ years of manned flight, we have identified, engineered, and/or trained away environmental threats that have killed better pilots than you. G-forces, hypoxia, and spatial disorientation are but a few of these threats and the professionals in Physiology will train you how to identify the hazards and take proven corrective actions that will keep you alive and let you complete the mission.

Physiology training will be a mixture of computer-aided instruction (get used to training via the computer), classroom instruction, and hands-on application. Additionally, if you suffer from airsickness in the T-6, these are the specialists that will give you the tools to overcome the pukes and keep you in flight school.

Physiology usually begins on day three of Phase I, immediately after your inprocessing briefings. Everyone in your class will be excited because you are finally wearing your flight suits every day and learning pilot stuff. The airmen in Physiology have the training down to an exact science and everything you learn is directly applicable to the flying arena. Over eight training days you will cover a variety of topics that will keep you alive and that is not an overstatement. If that is not enough motivation, you will be given three examinations on what you learn in Physiology--your first honest to God pilot training exams!

The first thing you will notice when you enter the Aerospace Physiology flight is the altitude chamber. Made of heavy steel and giant pipes, the chamber looks like a bank vault with old school, steam lever controls on the outside. As odd as it seems, the chamber will prepare you to operate in the high altitude environment. More on that later.

Physiology will also prepare you for the Air Force method for academic instruction--computer information to study in advance, classroom lecture, followed by hands-on training and ending in a real-world evaluation. Crawl, walk, and run is how the training is designed and you will see that system of teaching for the rest of your Air Force career.

Physiology is broken into three main blocks of instruction:

- Aerospace Physiology

- Survival

- Aircrew Flight Equipment

Aerospace Physiology--Aerospace Physiology covers the basic science of how the human body reacts to the flying environment. Despite all the poetry and dreams of mankind since the beginning of history, the human body is actually poorly designed for flying--probably because we have only been doing it for a hundred years or so. Having said that, the United States Air Force has been on the cutting edge of understanding and overcoming the physiological hazards of flying. The proof is how our training is copied by virtually every air force in the world today.

Survival--This is the catchall phrase that covers instruction in the skills of staying alive in case you have to leave your airplane. Your commissioning source sent you to basic survival training, so 80% of what you see is already familiar. The new instructional material revolves around the unique challenges of survival post aircraft exit. Nothing in this block of training is cosmic, and a lot will be common sense, like while flying in the U.S., carry your cell phone because it is a reliable form of communication in an emergency.

Aircrew Flight Equipment (AFE)--This block of training is fun and directly applies to activities you will do every day of your flying career. During this block you will get hands-on experience with your helmet and oxygen mask, so you need to make sure they are issued and fitted properly.

This is important--make sure you take your time, work with the professionals in AFE and physiology to get your flight gear fitted properly the first time. In the next few weeks, you are going to be putting your very best effort into your once-in-a-lifetime chance to become a USAF pilot. The last thing you want is a physical distraction of an ill-fitting helmet or an oxygen mask that sits on your face incorrectly. The same holds true for your harness and G-suit. Save yourself a ton of ass pain by getting your gear fitted right--how do you do this?

1. Schedule your appointment with aircrew flight equipment, arrive early (10 minutes is plenty), and have all the proper paperwork completed.

2. Be Nice! It sounds simple but you would be amazed how often students are rude to the support workers. Aside from the poor manners, it is just plain dumb. You are not pilots but you are acting cocky like you are one--you are not fooling anyone. Worst of all, you are being an ass to the people who fix and maintain the equipment that literally keeps you alive! See the problem?

3. Arrive with free time after your appointment. It is not unusual for the life support tech to be called away during your fitting to handle a problem with a pilot stepping out the door to a jet. The flyers on the way out the door always have priority, so you will wait while the problem is fixed. The active fliers have a takeoff time, you don't. If you are relaxed and not pressed for time, the tech will be helpful and patient. That is a win.

4. This is technique, but I always return later and bring a small gift after my fitting. Totally not required, but I ask the tech their favorite adult beverage. I go get it and hand-deliver it. No fanfare and absolutely no drama. These people work very hard for very little reward and they often get a lot of douchebag attitude from the aircrews. A kind word and a thoughtful gift goes a long way to make you stand out in a very positive way. A huge side benefit is that your gear will magically receive VIP treatment, and if you ever

have an issue with a piece of equipment, it will astonish you how fast you will move to the front of the line.

Once your gear is issued and properly fitted, you are ready for training.

In your first block of with aerospace physiology, you are introduced to the science of how the body reacts to the flying environment. You will learn the basic principles of the atmosphere, and have an introduction to basic human respiration, circulation, and orientation systems. Upon this foundation, you will then learn altitude-related threats including hypoxia, trapped gasses, and decompression sickness. Afterwards, you will see how human orientation feedback is exceeded during flight, and personally experience spatial disorientation in both the Barany Chair and Spatial Disorientation Trainer.

Barany Chair (U.S. Air Force photo/Senior Airman Frank Casciotta)

Spatial Disorientation (commonly referred to as Spatial D) is the inability to accurately orient yourself with respect to the earth's horizon. Believe it or not, during flight, your body will sense one thing, "I'm in a gentle turn to the right", and the instruments of the aircraft will tell you something totally different, "You are pointed straight at the ground and upside down." The Barany chair demos and Spatial Disorientation Trainer will allow you to experience this flight phenomenon in a safe environment and learn the prevention measures. It is the perfect opportunity to experience this disorientation and seeing your buddy's (victim's) face is hilarious.

Spatial Disorientation Trainer (U.S. Air Force photo/Staff Sergeant Nancy Falcon)

After your Aerospace Physiology test, you will learn some of the basic components of survival and personal protection in the event you have to leave your airplane. Sometimes this training includes a live fire flare-signaling demo with the MK-124.

Now that you are the survival expert, it is off into a deep-dive study of Air Force oxygen systems, the T-6 On-Board Oxygen Generating System (OBOGS), and hands-on oxygen equipment lab time to learn personal equipment components to include how to properly hook up your mask to the aircraft system. Once these fundamentals of equipment and oxygen systems are understood and practiced, students learn the components required for the operational checks of their oxygen system.

Next, you learn how to strap into and out of the T-6. (Incidentally, in between the T-6 phase and your follow-on aircraft, you will return to physiology to learn the oxygen system and egress procedures for your new airframe.) The egress (escape from) procedure in the T-6 is an important block of training, and you have plenty of opportunity to get comfortable with the proper steps. There are mock-up trainers in the physiology building, and you will have plenty of chances to practice the motor skills of strapping and unstrapping the aircraft. I know this sounds tedious and silly--why can't you just learn how to do this at the airplane? The reason is your time in the jet is incredibly valuable and limited. The amount of information and muscle memory you are responsible for is staggering. Strapping into and out of an airplane can be practiced in a building during office hours. The last thing anyone wants to do is waste time at the airplane learning how to hook up the G-suit. Time spent strapping in and out is time *not* spent learning the traffic pattern.

Another factor to remember, after your fourth or fifth flight in the T-6 - if you have a hard time getting ready to fly, it will frustrate your instructor pilot. Making the person teaching you to fly (and grading your performance) frustrated or mad is not a good idea. Finally, the muscle memory is important from an emergency procedures standpoint. Several emergency procedures conclude with an "emergency ground egress." This means you stop the jet, secure the engine and haul ass to a safe distance. Practice unstrapping from the jet is actually making you safer in the event of a real world crisis. Once your class is through this block of training, it is a good idea to find some time in your schedule and practice strapping into and out of the aircraft. The superstars at Aerospace Physiology will allow you to do this during normal duty hours. Get a couple of your buddies and practice this (helmet and oxygen mask too!) until it feels natural. While some guys in your class are studying how many rivets are on the airplane, you are spending a few hours becoming smooth at a task that makes your time at the actual jet more productive.

T-6 Texan parachute decent and landing training comes next and this block of instruction is a blast. Make sure someone brings a GoPro and cameras for these events. The procedures for ejection and what happens afterwards are the heart and soul of this phase. After the classroom instruction, the class will goes outside to an adult jungle gym playground of scaffolding and platforms to learn how to accomplish parachute landing falls (PLFs), the hanging harness, and parachute detaching procedures.

(U.S. Air Force photo/SrA Frank Casciotta)

- Parachute landing falls is the nice name we give to the Air Force-approved way of hitting the ground after bailing out of your airplane. The entire class will get the opportunity to stand on the platform and do PLFs until they are no longer fun. I won't bother explaining them to you here, because your instructors will teach you. Just do as you are taught and have fun with it. YouTube has tons of videos online that demonstrate the process. Also, these are the same basic procedures your great grandfather learned during World War II.

• The hanging harness is a fun, military version of the tire swing of your youth. Suspended from a high tower, you hang in your parachute harness and learn the procedures to accomplish if you are under a parachute (twisted harnesses, chute malfunctions, etc.). The idea is to prove to yourself that if you had to eject from a perfectly good aircraft, you would be ready. The harness itself is uncomfortable, because a couple of the straps jock up through your legs and nether regions (crotch). The hanging harness contraption drops you to the ground at a pretty exciting speed and gives you the chance to practice your PLF. If you are anything like me, you will hit toes, butt, and head to prove you didn't learn anything from the endless PLF drills.

• A real danger in the moments after a real-world parachute landing is being dragged, especially in the water. Nothing is worse than safely escaping a crippled aircraft and dying because you were dragged to your death by a wind-filled parachute that you cannot detach--it could drag you into the post-crash fire/wreckage. In the next block of training your class gets a chance to practice your detachment skills from the parachute harness, lying on your back in the field as two of your classmates drag you along behind them. It is good fun and great training, just make sure you take plenty of pictures, they make great Christmas card material. Make sure to get plenty of footage with the GoPro, the class videographer will use the footage for the videos later.

The altitude chamber demo is the culmination of your time with Aerospace Physiology. This chamber's pump system is able to induce barometric change comparable to aircraft ascent and descent rate. During the altitude chamber event, you will experience hypoxia symptoms at 25,000 feet above ground level (AGL), a visual acuity demo and a rapid decompression. The ride takes about 60-90 minutes depending on individual tolerance to hypoxia and if everyone can follow directions. My best advice to you is to listen to the instruction during the pre-brief and do what you are told once you are in the chamber.

Altitude Chamber (U.S. Air Force photo/Airman 1st Class Harry Brexel)

Once in chamber, the ride begins with the techs pumping out air from the container to simulate climbing in altitude. The first objective is an ear and sinus check. You go up to 5,000 feet to ensure the entire class is able to clear their ears. On ascent in flight, barometric pressure increases, requiring a "Valsalva" maneuver. The Valsalva works to equalize pressure in you middle ear by pinching your nose and forcefully exhaling against a closed airway (your mouth). This will result in a "popping" or an equalization of the pressure in the middle ear with the outside pressure.

Once you have accomplished the ear and sinus check, you begin to breathe 100% oxygen to reduce the risk of any decompression sickness. After the class completes 30 minutes of pre-breathing pure oxygen, the chamber will climb up to a simulated 25,000 feet for the hypoxia demonstration. On the way up to altitude you will start to feel the gasses in your guts start to expand--let them out! Massive flatulence is the order of the day, the fouler the better. Extra points if you ate Mexican food the night before.

The most deadly brew I ever experienced was from a couple of guys that had beer and pickled eggs the night before. Their noxious gases were pure sulfur, and let's just say that it was so bad, it made the paint on the chamber walls begin to bubble up.

Once you get to altitude, everyone drops his or her masks and this is the primary objective for the chamber ride. After a couple of minutes at that altitude, you will start to experience the symptoms of hypoxia. Everyone's personal symptoms of hypoxia are a little different, and the whole purpose of this demonstration is so that you can identify your symptoms in-flight. My symptoms are tingling in my fingertips and my nail beds turn blue. The purpose of this entire ride is to identify your symptoms of hypoxia and *take corrective action!* Failure to do this results in a loss of consciousness. It is funny in the chamber, but not so funny when it results in an aircraft mishap. Once you have identified your own hypoxia symptoms, you "gang load" your oxygen regulator (all three switches up--on/emergency pressure/100% O2) then swing your oxygen mask to your face. Sounds simple, but someone in your class will try and gut out the hypoxia. This is not why you are in the chamber! You are there to identify your personal symptoms and take corrective action--that is all. The "I'm tougher than everyone else" stuff will most likely result in the idiot passing out during the chamber flight. For this student, in addition to wasting everyone's time, a failure to recognize symptoms ensures a "re-do" of the chamber training. And a nice visit to the flight surgeon's office, because he lost consciousness.

After the hypoxia demo, the techs will drop you down to 18,000 feet and you will complete another demo to see how your visual acuity is affected in the high altitude environment.

The last task in the chamber is a rapid decompression demonstration. Within the chamber, pressure is dropped suddenly, which simulates a loss of pressurization (for example, a ruptured aircraft hull). The only trick here is to not to hold your breath. I kept my mouth slightly open during this event.

A fairly accurate and entertaining Hollywood version of the chamber ride is depicted in the movie, *"An Officer and a Gentleman."* I recommend you give it a look before physiology training.

After your chamber flight, you are done in Physiology and now it is on to T-6 academics!

ACADEMICS

A major portion of your time in Undergraduate Pilot Training will be spent in academics. There is an unbelievable amount of knowledge you must gain to be safe in the aviation arena and academics is the fire hose of knowledge you must learn to drink from if you hope to be successful. Academics is the catchall term used to describe the computer-aided instruction, classroom lecture, and tests you will take while in pilot training. Let me assure you, academic classes are very thorough on every subject given, to the point of being tedious. You will spend long hours in the computer lab and classroom getting knowledge drilled into your thick nugget. After class, you will spend even more hours every night going over the material you were just taught and reading ahead for the next block of instruction. As always, you biggest danger is not so much failing an individual test as it is to blow a test and that failure causing you to fall behind your classmates. An added stressor in this mixture is that three academic test failures triggers a Commander's Review (CR), which means you are going to the Wing Commander's office to determine if you will remain in flight school. Your odds of being reinstated at this point are, frankly, pretty low. In general, commanders and the Air Force have a very low tolerance for test failure because it is seen as laziness or unsuitability to the Air Force's flying culture.

The majority of academic instruction takes place in Phase I and II but there are a few areas of instruction and testing that roll into Phase III. Trust me, it is a milestone in Undergraduate Pilot Training when you take (and pass!) your final academic test. Rest assured, you will still have plenty of additional tests on the flight line, but we will cover that later.

During the Phase I and II you will have academic tests in the following subjects;

1. Joint Physiology

2. Life Support

3. Joint Survival

4. Weather *(One of the most difficult exams in UPT)*

5. T-6 Systems I

6. T-6 Systems II

7. T-6 Aerodynamics

8. Flying Fundamentals

9. Contact

10. Instruments I

11. Instruments II

12. Navigation

13. Formation

This list can seem daunting, but this gaggle just takes you to the end of Phase II.

AETC ACADEMIC TESTING

During your time at Undergraduate Pilot Training, you will be evaluated almost on a daily basis. Each flight maneuver, Stand Up, and Bold Face/Ops Limits tests are all ways you are measured. A major portion of your evaluation is the academic tests you take at Undergraduate Pilot Training. Air Education and Training Command (AETC) has developed its testing methods over many decades and frankly, there are some tricks to the system that will help you be successful. Pay attention to these facts and you will do just fine.

There are 17 academic tests administered in USAF pilot training. All the tests are multiple-choice exams (normally four possible answers) and you will take them on a computer-based testing system. Minimum passing score is 85% for all tests.

Don't fail a test (obviously), it will cost you extra time to go over the failed test material. An instructor, by regulation, has to walk you through each missed question and explain why your answer was wrong, retrain you in the subject matter, and have you retake the exam. You should be using that time to hammer your Boldface/Ops Limits or practice Stand Up, NOT going over old ground. Add in the stress of a failure and you are putting yourself on the road to washing out. Perfection is always the goal, but 85% is passing and passing is good enough.

Fail the retest and now you are running onto dangerous ground. Two failures instantly land you in the Commanders Awareness Program (CAP) for academics. This keeps the squadron leadership up to speed on your progress. Being on CAP puts unwanted focus on you--avoid it.

This is the most important thing I can tell you about academics in pilot training. Memorize this test taking acronym--RTFQ/RTFA and you will do fine. It stands for READ THE FUCKING QUESTION, READ THE FUCKING ANSWER. I lived this acronym every time I sat for an exam and it works. For some reason, students try to rush through the tests and forget to follow the basics. They breeze through part of the question, see an answer that has some of the correct wording they were looking for, click it and move on--boom, swing and a miss, enjoy the retest. Read the entire question carefully, completely and read all the answers, even if you see the correct one, right away--read them all. The tests are all timed but I have never seen anyone not complete them. You have plenty of time to complete the tests, use it.

AETC is famous for their tests for good reason. The typical question will have a clear, correct answer but the multiple choices can be tricky. Aside from the correct answer, another will be very close to the right answer, a third may be the correct verbiage but exactly opposite of the intent, and very rarely is the fourth answer an obvious throw away. The tests are subtle and it takes a while to get the hang of them.

Also, don't delve too deeply into the individual subjects--the computer-based training and your instructors will teach to the level of knowledge you need. You are here to earn your pilot wings, wasting class time to explain the laws of thermodynamics to the instructor/class pisses everyone off and doesn't get you extra credit. Also, UPT is not like college. You will be given information in the computer training and in the manuals/publications that will be on the test. Your instructor may not go over that information in class--you are still responsible to know it! Whining that you failed a test because your instructor did not teach you something is not an answer.

There was a guy in my class who was a no-shit rocket scientist. He said being selected for pilot training was his reward for his engineering work on nuclear missiles. This guy spent the year trying to prove how much smarter he was than everyone else so he would waste class time by yammering on and on about jet engine and rocket theory. Everybody hated his guts, instructors included, by the time we hit the flight line. I finished higher in the academic ranking than he did. Why? Not because I was smarter than he was, but because I learned to concentrate my study time and effort, give back the knowledge the instructors taught me, and hit the books. He barely made it through because he spent his time quibbling about small points of engineering and not trying to learn the information for flying. The knowledge you learn is so you can safely fly, it is a means to an end, not the reason you are at UPT. Stay in your lane, focus on getting the information, and you will be happy.

Do not apply any outside knowledge to the tests. Nobody cares that you majored in meteorology in college and specialized in thunderstorms.

When the test question asks for the three elements that lead to T-storm formation, just answer with what the instructor or the computer taught you. If it is not in your learning material or you haven't heard it in class, you have not been taught it and it will not be on the test, period. You are not here to change the system, just show learned knowledge.

Testing can be a very straightforward part of pilot training and the knowledge you gain is important. That said, it is a threat and from time to time students wash out because of poor testmanship. Apply the rule-- RTFQ/RTFA and you will kick ass in academics.

CHEATING

As an Air Force pilot, your reputation is everything. It may sound like a war movie cliché, but day in and day out you will literally put your life in the hands of others. You have to know that the pilots around you will not cut corners and jeopardize the mission and your life. So what happens when you know the pilot you are relying on is a known cheater? What happens when you climb onto a jet as a passenger and see the class cheater at the controls?

Since time began, people have cheated on tests and gotten away with it. When I was a line instructor, I saw students cheat and they all eventually got caught. The students usually fell into two camps, the students that cheated and those that looked down on them because of it. Aside from that, if you get caught cheating, you are out of flight school, period.

Any quick Google search on Air Force and cheating will show you a ton of articles about the cheating scandal that occurred in the nuclear mission. How did that work out for everybody involved?

One last thought on this subject, if you decide to cheat, make sure you own it. By that I mean, if you are going to taint your reputation, be honest to yourself that you are doing it. If you get caught, please take responsibility for being a dirt bag. Don't blame anyone else, whine that everybody is cheating, or cry that you didn't know better. Own your failure and just resign from flight school before you can be kicked out. Maybe you can find some other career that suits your earned reputation.

130

CLASS PATCH AND VIDEO

Two Undergraduate Pilot Training traditions are your class patch and the videos your class will show during track and assignment night. Every year, one or two classes will have trouble getting these tasks accomplished and the accompanying drama completing them takes time away from your primary job--graduating from flight school. Follow this guidance, get them done drama free, and save your classmates the hassle.

Class Patch--Patches and aviation go hand in hand and have been a part of the heritage since the get-go. You *will* have a patch, so get it done. Your class will be tasked with designing a patch, getting it approved by leadership, having the patch massed produced, and making a "patch board" which is a large image of your classes' patch that will be hung on the wall. This is a perfect opportunity for everybody to work together and help the cause, so make sure to do your part, plus a little more.

Design--If you have someone in your class who can draw, terrific, that person just became the official artist for the class. If they do their job correctly, it will only take a few hours. First off, no one cares what your patch looks like unless it is sexist, racist, or has any copyrighted material.

Stay away from those three bogies and you are golden. The first two for obvious reasons, the last one is because of the copyright laws. Someone will have to write to the owner of the copyrighted property and get permission to use it--delay and drama for something that does not matter. Make sure the artist does not get too fine with the detail, the subtle features and colors will not transfer to the cloth of a patch. Your base will have hundreds of examples everywhere to give you inspiration.

If no one in you class can draw, go onto the internet and find free symbols and shapes to use. Point, click, and add text and you are done. What could be simpler than that?

Get the patch made--Now that you have the patch design, you need to get it approved and produced. Once everyone has agreed to the design, it is submitted to the Sturon for approval, and then someone in the class volunteers to place the order. This takes money and it is time for the class to pony up. More colors equals more expensive to make, so that should be a consideration in the design. The student squadron will have plenty of experience with getting patches made, so use the resources available to you, don't reinvent the wheel. There may be a local vendor the student squadron likes to use or there are tons of places listed on the internet. Personally, I got 50 patches for myself and I had plenty left over at the end of training. Do not let this project hang around. Remember, at the same time this happens you are trying to learn the Boldface/Ops Limits of the T-6. Find a vendor, place the order and close the deal. You will need about 10 class patches with Velcro attached for your flight suit. Either order some of the patches with Velcro or find a local vendor that will sew them on for you. You will be surprised how many people "borrow" your class patch right off your shoulder, so have extras in a stash at home.

CLASS VIDEOS

Twice during the year, the class will have major milestone events that the entire flight school is invited to attend--track select night and assignment night. I will explain these two events in much greater detail later. On both occasions the class is responsible for providing the opening entertainment and this takes the form of a class video. The two videos should last two to five minutes (about the length of the background song) and provide a humorous glimpse of your time in the various phases of pilot training. Okay, you know what is expected so get to it!

• Pick someone in your class to be the videographer. With all the technology available these days--cell phones, GoPro, etc.--it is a pretty simple job. Start recording the events in Phase I. Standard fare for this are PLFs, parachute release, hanging harness, and the altitude chamber. Pass the camera around and make sure there is plenty of footage.

• Once you have the physiology events documented, plan on taking footage for a few minutes each week. Make sure to capture your classmates getting tossed into the solo tank!

• Finally add in some flying and formation footage. There is a ton of material on the Internet or you can go through the steps to get permission to carry a GoPro on the jet.

• About a week prior to track and assignment night, have two classmates sit down a splice a video together. Most classes put the video to a single song so you only need enough to cover that time period.

Don't think that your class will be able to skip out on this requirement. It is a tradition and you do not want your class to get the reputation of being lazy or difficult. The flight commander for your class will give you the guidelines on how to make the videos. Word to the wise--be very careful with humor. The Air Force has no sense of humor when it comes to inappropriate videos. As a safe rule of thumb, if you wouldn't show it to your grandmother, you probably shouldn't show it during track select or assignment night.

DECOMPRESS

As I have said many times throughout this book, UPT is stressful both mentally and physically. You are thrust into a totally alien environment and hammered constantly to perform at a world-class level. All that tension must have an outlet or you will pop. Prior to entering flight school, you will have plenty of time to develop outside hobbies and interests. Take it from me, you need the opportunity to drop everything and blow off steam. If you don't take some time off and try to live some sort of "warrior monk" lifestyle, it will work for a while and then you will burn out, literally and figuratively. Develop hobbies and interests while on the break between college and flight school, focusing on interests that get you away from the base and the military.

My personal recommendation is to avoid hobbies and sports that are bad for your health, are expensive, or that are location limited. The first is obvious but it is amazing how many lieutenants blindly fall into the other two types. For example, if you hell bent to take up surfing or heli-skiing, go for it, those are amazing and fun sports. Also, they are hellishly expensive and dependent on locations and opportunity. The last time I checked there are no USAF pilot training bases within easy driving distances of these sports. Do you want to spend all your down time traveling to your pressure relief or spend it relieving the pressure? Further, the chance of injury in these sports is pretty high so make sure you are making good choices. Better choices would be running, biking--both road and mountain, and any kind of gym workout that you enjoy.

Remember, the criteria are;

- Something you enjoy

- Relatively good for you or at least not obviously bad for your health

- Away from the base and military

- Inexpensive

- Easy access and hours

While on the subject, let's discuss a reasonable work/study schedule. Unless the flying program on your base becomes very far behind the training timeline, your days will be limited to 12 hours, Monday--Friday. Weekends, federal holidays, and AETC down days are off. As the weeks go by in training, it is critical for you to establish a healthy routine where you are getting in the proper amount of study, training, and rest. Get one segment out of whack and you are headed for a fall. When I say 12-hour days, I mean expect to be in a class or the flight room for a full 12 hours. Commute time does not count in this calculation, so a 5-minute walk to your UOQ takes on added value.

Everyone has to find the right rhythm for him or herself when it comes to UPT. Here are the general guidelines I kept for myself:

- Out of bed one hour prior to the daily show time, look over my flashcards as I get ready for work and eat.

- Make sure I arrive at the right location ten minutes before show time.

- Any breaks during the day are golden chances to play pop quiz with my classmates.

- After work, head straight back to the room, don't BS in the parking lot with your classmates.

- Dinner is eating and studying on your own.

- Most every night was chairflying and group study with my buds from class. Bedtime is already planned and scheduled, do not break this routine!

- In bed on time, every night. Personally, I need seven hours of rack time to perform at my best, this is just as important as eating and study.

- Friday night, goof off (drink, play grab ass, whatever) with your class.

- Saturday, no study at all. Go do something away from the base and flying, preferably away from your classmates.

- Sunday morning, slept in as much as I could and cleaned up my room. Laundry and shopping for the week ahead.

- Sunday afternoon, watch sports while studying. At 1800, the weekend was over and balls-to-the-wall all over again.

- Repeat!

Sounds boring, I know, but this is the kind of hard work and routine that gets great results. When you get frustrated with the routine just remember two things, once you graduate you can make up for all the lost time you had in flight school, and *why are you here*?

Save going out of town for long weekends and holidays. Make sure to know and follow the rules for travel, when you need a pass or take leave. Don't mess around with these rules--follow them to the letter. Remember, the Air Force has not invested a lot of money in you yet, so tossing you out of flight school for someone who can't follow the rules is super easy.

Additionally, depending on the flying timeline, most UPT bases shut down flying and training in late December (21, 22, 23 Dec) and do not reopen until after the New Year (2,3,4 Jan). Take leave and get out of town! The Undergraduate Pilot Training system is not built for you to be hanging around anyway, so go somewhere. Otherwise, if you insist on staying on station you will be tagged with reporting in on certain occasions and doing worthless additional duties. You need this time to recharge your mental batteries to survive the crappy deep winter weather flying, so go do something fun.

Now Undergraduate Pilot Training is rolling for real. Every day you wake up, you are one day closer to waking across that stage. So far the training and the pace has been pretty easy, but now the train is about to pick up steam. The end of Phase I means you and your class on headed to the flight line and the T-6 Texan. Pilot training is about to become very real--on to Phase II!

UPT--PHASE II

Phase II
Scheduled length = 90 flying training days or 28 calendar weeks
Programed flight hours = 87
Academic tests = 11 (Weather, T-6 Systems I & II, Aerodynamics, Flying Fundamentals, Contact, Instruments I II & III, Navigation, Formation)
Checkrides = Mid-Phase, Final Contact, Instrument, and Formation
Milestones = Dollar Ride, Solo out, Solo tank toss, Mid-Phase check, Formation flight, Track Night

Phase II is the best and worst of times at Undergraduate Pilot Training. It is fantastic because you are finally actually flying and training to become a real pilot and terrible because the pressure and stress of pilot training reaches its highest levels. All your hard work and the hours of studying are about to pay off! The objective of this phase is to establish the foundation of the "Air Force way of flying." It may sound like an odd expression, but there is truth to the term. The Air Force has a very specific approach to the science and art of aviation. You will learn the AF way of flying or you will be gone. I have personally witnessed a UPT student with over 3,000 hours of civilian flight time wash out. He was dismissed not because he could not fly but because he refused to adjust his methods of aviation to the Air

Force standard. Get with the program or get out, it is that simple.

As a side note, this phase of training has the highest wash out rate in Undergraduate Pilot Training.

Phase II continues the fire hose of information with academics and now the added effect of daily life on the flight line.

Over the years, I have been asked if entering flight school with a lot of flight hours in civilian aviation will help candidates get their wings. As with most military questions, the answer is "Yes, but…"

Arriving at UPT with a lot of civilian flight hours will definitely help you in the beginning of pilot training and especially in Phase II. Having said that, I have witnessed two individuals begin flight school in the same class, worlds apart in terms of civilian flight time--thousands vs. zero. The person with a lot of flight time did better initially than the person with zero flight hours, but by the end of T-6's both were equal in ability. In a nutshell, that speaks to the effectiveness and "leveling" of Undergraduate Pilot Training.

EP Quizzes--EPQ's

Arriving at the flight line introduces you to squadron life and Emergency Procedures Quizzes. If you hate the academic tests, you are going to absolutely loathe EP Quizzes and you will see them until you graduate from pilot training. EP Quizzes are given once per week (usually Monday or Friday) and consist of 25 multiple-choice questions--85% is passing. The flight line and academics do not de-conflict their schedules, so you can rest assured that sometime during UPT your class will have an EP Quiz and an academic test on the same day--probably more than once. Bust the EP Quiz and you sit for the day. Further, EPQ's scores are calculated into your overall class ranking (meritocracy!) so your scores affect your future assignments.

Also, to add to the fun of Phase II, there is a super EP Quiz that consists of 50 questions and you must pass this test before you can take your mid-phase checkride.

General Knowledge vs. Junk Knowledge (aka, stupid airplane trivia)-- There is a difference between studying for general knowledge and chasing junk knowledge and it is important to differentiate between the two. General knowledge is the study and retention of information that helps you operate the airplane safely and efficiently and/or that might be asked of you during a checkride. Junk knowledge is the pursuit of worthless trivia that does not increase your ability to safely operate the aircraft or successfully pass a checkride. For example:

GK information--What is the flap limit speed of the aircraft?

Junk Knowledge--How many rivets are on the airplane?

Many times, you will see UPT students show off their trivia knowledge at the expense of general knowledge. Don't do this--pay attention to what is important and the trivia heads get hammered in their mid-phase ground evaluation.

(U.S. Air Force photo by Master Sgt. David Richards)

THE T-6 TEXAN II

In the late 1990s, the Air Force realized that the venerable T-37 "Tweets" were well past their service life and were in desperate need of replacement. After the normal drama and delay associated with the military acquisition process, the Beechcraft T-6 Texan II was finally identified and fully fielded in the early 2010s. Although it is a turbo-prop aircraft, it is light years ahead of the T-37 in reliability, capability, and (to be honest) comfort. Previous generations of student pilots stewed in their own sweat under that cursed "batman" bubble canopy of the old Tweets and cussed that shitty little air conditioning port. That worthless vent opened up to about the size of a nickel and blew a mild breeze of medium-warm air on the only exposed skin you had, the little patch below your jaw line and above your collar. That cockpit was easily over 110 degress and the only relief was that miserable, tiny gasper that was designed and built before my dad was in high school! Although it is always a little sad to see any old jets go to the boneyard, it was past time for the Tweets to leave the training arena.

(U.S. Air Force photo/Rick Johnson)

Comparatively, the T-6 is not even in the same discussion as the old T-37. Based on the design of the Pilatus PC-9, the Texan will remind you at first glance of the World War II era P-51 fighter. It is a proven training aircraft, safe and reliable. Although the T-6 is a primary training aircraft, the comparison between the T-6 and T-37 does not end there:

- The T-6 is pressurized and the air conditioning works like a champ, basically opposite of the T-37. In fact, the environmental controls are so effective, the pilots close the canopy during ground operations.

- The T-6 fields advanced ejection seats and you wear G-suits. In the old days we had to carry our parachutes (40 pounds) out to the T-37, now the parachute is contained in the ejection seat--you just wear a harness to the aircraft.

- The T-37 had a very slow and scary throttle delay, the T-6 does not. What this means is that when you pushed the power up in the T-37 you could literally count to three very slowly before those old, slow engines started pumping out power. It does not sound like a big problem, sitting in an easy chair at home, but it is too thrilling of a delay when you are out of airspeed and ideas, 50 feet over the runway and the only way to save your life is to jam the throttles forward as hard as humanly possible. In comparison, the T-6 Texan's thrust output is exhilarating. Jam the throttle forward and plenty of power is at your fingertips. The airplane literally leaps forward! Touch and gos are completed in mere tens of feet and you do not need to change the configuration of the airplane to accomplish the go around--unlike the Tweet.

If it sounds like I am harping about the discomfort of flying the T-37, I am. Aside from sweating your ass off in the jet, that kind of environment did not help you learn the art of aviation. In some ways I can argue we learned to fly despite the T-37.

As a measure of the U.S. dominance in the air, the T-6 is a training aircraft in the United States, but its variants are cutting-edge attack and fighter aircraft in other parts of the world. What other countries use to defend their nations, we use as a basic trainer! Manufactured by Beechcraft, the Texan is the perfect platform to take you from Joe Bag of Doughnuts to world-class aviator. Easy to operate, the Texan is a fantastic learning platform, and it will become your first true love. If I could keep an airplane in my garage to go chase clouds, it would be the T-6, hands down.

Here are the basic statistics on the T-6 Texan:

Manufacturer--Beechcraft

Crew--Two, pilots sit in tandem

Length--33ft, 4in

Wingspan--33ft, 5in

Maximum Airspeed--320 miles per hour

Maximum Altitude--31,000 feet

Range--900 nautical miles

(U.S. Air Force photo/Vance AFB Public Affairs)

Phase II is divided up into three separate blocks of training--contact, instrument and formation. Along the way you will get four checkrides to ensure you have learned the material in each particular area (two in the contact block).

CONTACT BLOCK

The contact block of training is the basic instruction that teaches you how to walk out to the airplane and prepare it to fly--taxi, takeoff, go to the practice area for aerobatics, return to the airfield, land safely, and park the jet. Everything that is required to operate the plane, beginning to end, is covered in detail, and this is what you will be evaluated in during your Mid-phase and Final Contact checkrides. It all begins with the dollar ride!

DOLLAR RIDE

You made it to your first ride in the T-6 Texan! Congratulations, not many people have made it this far in their aviation career. I won't get to specific on how this flight will go, because your training and chairflying will lay the groundwork for what you will actually accomplish during this flight. What I will mainly discuss are the good-to-know items and the little things that make your IP happy.

The old Chinese adage that the journey of a thousand miles begins with the first step applies to your dollar ride. The Air Force dutifully logs the all the flight time data and you can look back over 30 years to see that first day's details.

Since this is your first flight as an Air Force pilot, it is important to listen to your body and try to enjoy the ride. For the first and last time in your aviation career, you are not expected to know or be able to do virtually anything on an aircraft sortie.

Having said that, there are a few things to know before you go flying for the first time:

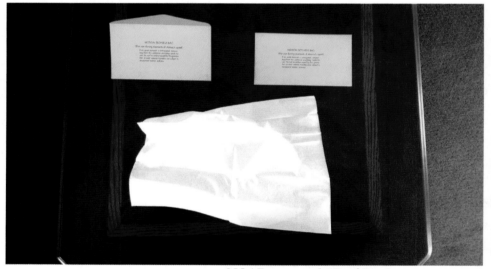

USAF approved "Barf Bag"

1. Make sure to eat a couple of hours before your flight. Everyone is trying to avoid becoming airsick and some idiot from your class will tell you not to eat to keep from puking. Stupid idea, having food in your belly makes you able to avoid being sick. Plus you won't be hungry and weak on that first flight. Obviously, do not stuff yourself and avoid a heavy, greasy meal before you step out

to the airplane.

2.   Take some of your own time at physiology in the days leading up to your flight and practice getting into and out of the jet, including strapping and unstrapping--completely. At least having an idea how to do this task will make your IP very happy.

3.   Relax! You will not bust this ride so enjoy the view. Everything will seem to come too fast and you will be overwhelmed--everyone feels that way! Despite what your instructor says, you are not the worst student the Air Force has ever seen.

4.   Maneuvers will be pretty vanilla (basic, bland) so that you can adapt to the flying environment. Concentrate on listening to your instructor and try to identify a few landmarks in the local area.

5.   Be a sponge! Your IP will give you plenty of information and demonstrate everything you need to learn. The quicker you learn, the happier everyone will be.

6.   Two barf bags, one out of the envelope and under your leg, number two in your pocket--just in case.

7.   If you feel sick--*say something!* The IP's goal on the dollar ride is to ensure you do not get airsick! Every instructor has techniques and tricks to help you feel better. S/he can't help you if they don't know you are feeling queasy.

One last word from an old pilot--keep your own flight records! The flight records office will keep good records, but good people sometimes make mistakes. Once a month--throughout your career, cross check the official record and your personal notes. If you catch the mistakes early, they are easy to fix. It would be a shame to "lose" a few hundred hours of flight time simply because of a counting mistake. In the aviation world, flight hours equate to experience and you must have a certain amount of hours to attend advanced schools and upgrades in the future.

THE AUXILIARY FIELD

The main focus of T-6 operations is to teach you the proper approach and landing procedures. This is the basis for all aviation and where a tremendous amount of effort and resources are directed. To that end, UPT bases utilize auxiliary fields. These are simply small runways usually located 30-40 miles from the base. These fields normally only operate during daylight, VFR (visual flight rules) operations. The biggest benefit of these airports is that they allow multiple approach and landing operations just for the T-6s. You will go to this field nearly every sortie during the contact block of T-6 training. Therefore, the procedures on how to travel to and operate in these aux fields must be near the top of your study/chairflying priorities. Just so you know, if you get lost going to the auxiliary field, you automatically fail the checkride!

Once you complete the dollar ride, UPT goes into high gear and you must begin to make progress in learning your profession. The contact training block specifies that you will fly or complete a simulator nearly every day. The program accelerates rapidly and you are expected to solo out in the T-6 in 12 aircraft sorties and before using 20 hours of flight time. In addition to the focus on take offs and landings, you will see a marked increase in the amount and difficulty of the aero-work conducted in the training areas. A typical sortie in these blocks will consist of:

- Take off and departure from the home airport

- Flight to the auxiliary air field for multiple approaches

- Entry into the training areas for aerobatics and training maneuvers

- Return to the home base

- Multiple approaches and landings until time and or fuel

requires a full stop

Solo out

Your first solo in the T-6 is an exciting flight and a sortie you will remember forever. To reach this milestone, your instructor pilot must feel you can safely accomplish a few tasks:

1. Take off and land consistently

2. Operate safely in the traffic pattern

3. If an emergency occurred, can you safely put the jet on the ground?

4. Can you see when an unsafe situation develops during approaches and make the smart decision to just go around?

It is really just that simple and this is where the hours of study and chairflying really pay off.

The actual sortie is very straightforward. Normally, the flight is planned as a pattern only flight. You will execute multiple take offs and landings, usually three safe ones in a row. Additionally, you get to accomplish a break out of the traffic pattern and a normal re-entry. Once your IP feels that you are not too much of a danger to yourself or anyone else, s/he will tell you to go back to parking and after engine is shutdown, s/he will secure the backseat of your T-6 and you are on your own. After that is complete, you will go through all the normal start-up, taxi out and take off procedures.

I remember my first solo flight - the feeling of joy and accomplishment is hard to describe. Best of all, there is no instructor pilot in your ear telling you all the things you are doing wrong. Then again, there is no instructor pilot back there to fix things if you screw up! There is a slight feeling of anxiety knowing that you and only you control everything.

The main difference in military and civilian solo flights is the speed in which you are expected to reach that level of training. In the civilian world, the standard of training is until your instructor feels comfortable, so therefore some people never solo. In UPT the syllabus calls for you to solo after 15 flight hours--drinking from a fire hose!

After three touch and gos by yourself, it is all over and you taxi back to parking--get ready for your dunking!

Vance AFB Class 16-13, Capt Vitaliy Benz

SOLO DUNK TANK

Just like your class patch, the solo dunk tank is a fun rite of passage of your time in pilot training. Each base does the solo tank a little different but in general the solo dunk tank is a metal cattle-watering tank about 12 feet in diameter and two feet deep. The solo tank is normally set up between life support and the flying squadron. Each class gets to paint the tank to its own taste. This usually involves a party on a weekend just after the prior class completes all its solo flights.

The rules of the dunk tank vary, but basically when you solo out in the

T-6, your classmates wait to ambush you as you return to the flight room. Once grabbed, you have a chance to remove your boots and empty your pockets--then it is one, two, three, and in you go. The outside temperature does not matter and you get extra points if they have to break ice to get you dunked. Make sure plenty of people take video and pictures because this moment is perfect fodder for track and assignment night.

MID-PHASE CONTACT CHECKRIDE

After your solo flight in T-6, you will see a marked acceleration of the training program. You will be expected to go to the mid-phase check in five aircraft sorties after the solo out. This is a perfect snapshot of the murderous pace of Phase II.

The instructor pilots and the training syllabus begin to focus on preparing you for your first Air Force checkride--the dreaded mid-phase check. This checkride has the dubious honor of having the most number of unsatisfactory (failure) grades earned in any check at UPT--40+%. Also, the majority of people who wash out of pilot training begin to stumble in the rides leading up to mid-phase.

Mid-phase is focused on safety in the traffic pattern, launch, and recovery of the aircraft. The balance of your study preparation should not be in perfecting your aerobatics but in traffic pattern operations. The old saying we had when I was a line instructor pilot--*no one busts mid-phase check because of an ugly loop, but lots of people bust for forgetting their flaps on a touch and go*--still applies.

Put your study time on general knowledge, departure and recovery, and the auxiliary field operations. Most people earn their Unsats due to poor risk management and decision areas of the checkride.

Quick points to remember before going into your mid-phase checkride:

• Do not force a bad situation. If you make a bad final turn, don't try to save it, go around! This falls into the decision-making arena. The check pilot is more interested that you made the smart decision and went around rather than trying to save a bad approach.

• Be conservative. If you need to add a little power for the simulated engine out approach, add it. If you start to enter an aerobatic maneuver and realize it will take you out of the training area (automatic bust), break off the maneuver and re-accomplish it!

• Something will happen during this checkride that you do not expect, I guarantee it! If the check pilot were not there, how would you deal with the unexpected problem? If you need help, ask for it but not from your check pilot. Go as if the CP were not there but include him/her in the decision-making process. Tell the check pilot what decisions you are making and why.

• Use your radio to help you--if you need it. If you are confused or unsure of something, it is okay to call the Supervisor of Flying (SOF) and ask a question. Same thing with Air Traffic Control (ATC) and the Runway Supervisory Unit (RSU) controller. When in doubt, speak plain English on the radio.

• Put in the study time to nail your Pre-mission Briefing and General Knowledge. I have been the check pilot on scads of checkrides over the years and two universal truth shines through; 1) Bad briefing = bad checkride. 2) If the student is weak on General Knowledge, they are showing me that they do not care about their checkride.

Mid-phase checkride is a big (painful) milestone in your pilot training and you will be happy/relieved when it is over. You will not get a chance to catch your breath before it is time to get ready for the next meat grinder, Final Contact checkride.

FINAL CONTACT CHECK

This checkride is almost a carbon copy of the mid-phase checkride, but you add in simulated emergency pattern work, more aerobatics and a lot more general pattern work. Frankly, if you can pass the mid-phase, final contact is pretty easy. The main difference is you are expected to make good decisions and entering all the maneuvers at the proper airspeed and altitude are key indicators that you are on track. As expected in all checkrides, you must prepare yourself mentally and physically to ensure you deliver an excellent sortie when the time comes.

Each block of instruction continues with additional maneuvers and landing requirements being added to each flight. Once you get comfortable, the Air Force adds additional requirements. All the universal truths of checkrides continue so read over that section and the mid-phase discussion before the final contact check.

INSTRUMENTS AND THE INSTRUMENT CHECK

The foundations of instrument flying are literally written in blood. Since the beginning of manned flight, flying at night and bad weather have killed better pilots than you. The Air Force has been on the forefront of procedures and technology to lessen the hazards but what you learn in Phase II of UPT is the bedrock of what you will use throughout your aviation career. Simply put, once you are a C-17 pilot, the nuances of landing a T-6 will fade from your memory but you will apply the instrument procedures you learned in the Texan every single day.

You will have plenty of simulator and aircraft sorties to teach you the instrument cross check and the procedures to safely operate in bad weather. No matter how much flying experience you have entering flight school, follow the instruction/procedures you are given. This is the phase where the students who enter UPT with a lot of flying hours (and poor habits) fall on their face. Generally, these students were taught bad procedures and they are not able to adapt to the new system. The Air Force method is tried and true: fine-tune your operating methods to the AF system and you will do just fine.

On the checkride, just remember: you are given a minimal number of

flights and simulators to learn instrument flying. Because of this it is easy
to be given a clearance on the radio that you have never heard before or
that you don't have properly set up. Don't panic! Ask for a new clearance,
play dumb on the radio, and speak plain English to get what you want or
clear the confusion.

FORMATION

Formation flying is just plain fun and exciting. For the first time in
your aviation career you will be flying in close proximity to another aircraft
(intentionally!) and operating as a team of two pilots to safely fly a specific
profile, together. Formation is undoubtedly the biggest difference between
civilian and military aviation. All military pilots have the ability to operate
safely within a few feet of another aircraft and perform maneuvers. The
biggest key to remember about formation is to--**Relax**. I know that it is
easier said than done, but the more relaxed you are on the controls, the
smoother you will be. Everyone has different techniques to achieve this
but I always tell my students to wiggle their toes. It works because it makes
you release the tension in your muscles and prevents over-controlling.

Formation consists of operating as a team from ground operations,
through a flight where you conduct a few aerobatic maneuvers, accomplish
break ups and rejoins, and then safely recover to the airfield as a team.
During all the sorties, you will have the opportunity to lead the formation
and after the "lead" switches, fly on the wing as wingman. The other
student will also be training to their new role and the more communication
you can develop with your counterpart, the better. By and large, you do
not know with whom in your class you will be paired with during your
formation flights (as you approach the checkride, the schedulers will try to
team up pairs of students for the sake of communication and continuity),
so your efforts to be a great classmate with a fantastic reputation really
pays off. Also, your efforts to get along with everyone in your class are
vindicated as well. You may not like the guy in the other jet, in fact you
may hate his guts, but you better be able to work together--you both have

a checkride to pass.

At its essence, formation is just like the contact phase of T-6 flying but now you are responsible for a second aircraft, during the contact ride. Failure to stay in the assigned airspace (this comes from not giving yourself

enough room to complete a maneuver or a rejoin) is a major reason students bust rides in Form phase.

(U.S. Air Force photo/SSgt Matthew Hannen)

FORMATION CHECKRIDE

By now in the Undergraduate Pilot Training program, you have seen three (at least) checkrides and have a basic grasp on how to pass an evaluation. Formation checkride is no exception to any of the other checkrides that you have seen so far. As usual, preparation is the key to a successful check and if you find yourself doing something brand new during your checkride--STOP!

Formation check is the culmination of Phase II and your time in the T-6. Takeoff and landings must be second nature by now and smooth operations as both leader and wingman are key to success. Honestly, the standard for passing the T-6 Formation phase is low and as long as the students don't do anything hugely scary (try to hit each other, lose each other on a rejoin, or bust out of the airspace they are operating in), both will pass the checkride in fine style.

Chairflying the check profile as a team will pay off handsomely on checkride day. With your assigned wingman, sit side by side and go over the entire sortie one step at a time. Practice radio calls and hand signals for every maneuver and operation you will do during the sortie. Try to throw the other guy off by tossing in random changes so you complicate the scenario. Since you are together, switch off who is lead and who is #2--you will both have a chance to lead during the check. The key is to build up that verbal and non-verbal communication to make checkride day even easier.

During the checkride itself, there is plenty of time and fuel to complete the flying profile so take your time on the profile and enter each maneuver in the perfect parameters. For example, once you travel out to the training airspace, do not rush into your maneuver profile. Have a steady deliberate pace to your profile--get established in the area, enter the first maneuver perfectly on speed, once completed, check the area boundaries, begin the next maneuver, and repeat until the profile is complete. Just like the mid-phase check, you won't bust the ride for an ugly loop but you will definitely bust it for going out of the training airspace.

Since there is plenty of fuel and time during this sortie, if you are doing well, the check pilots will take some of the flying time once your profiles are complete. This is a very good thing and you want the check pilots to fly as much as possible. If they ask you if you want to fly additional maneuvers in the area or any additional touch and goes beyond the profile--the answer is a very polite "No Sir/Ma'am, Thank you." *The reason is, if you are flying beyond your check profile and make a mistake (roll off the perch and forget to lower the gear) you bust the ride. Never mind that you just flew a perfect pattern five minutes before, too bad, so sad.*

Things to remember for your Formation Checkride;

- Traffic patterns, approach, and landings are the number one reasons students bust the formation checkride. They are so focused on the formation that they forget how to properly land the airplane. Don't let this happen to you! Also, don't relax in the traffic pattern when the formation breaks up for pattern work--you are still on the checkride.

• As lead, watch the area boundaries in all three dimensions. Before every maneuver, check your position in the area before starting the move.

• Stay in the area. Even if you are approaching a boundary, turn as needed to stay in the area. Even if you are being a "rough" leader, it is better to abuse the wingman a little (it is graded under "wingman consideration") than bust the whole checkride by flying too gently and exiting the area boundary.

TRACK SELECT NIGHT!

Closing out the T-6 phase of flight school is track select night! This is a giant milestone on your journey to the silver wings and a time to pat yourself on the back. Also, this is a massive pivot point in your life. Sometimes there are anxieties associated with this night because your performance will be measured in public and that can be a pop to the nose of your ego.

Every squadron and base conducts the track select night event a little differently, so take this description with a grain of salt.

Track select is a family affair and usually takes place later in the afternoon. Normally, the class orders up plenty of food and drinks for the crowd and has a social hour before the festivities begin. Once everything is set, the class lines up in the hallway and marches into an auditorium and is on one side of the room. The projector screens are on and the two flight commanders emcee the event. The class has a video to show and it depicts the individual members going through the more memorable highlights of Phase I and II. This includes the funny parts of physiology, parachute landing practice and being tossed into the dunk tank after your solo out.

Afterwards, each student is brought forward. His/her picture is put up on the screen and the flight instructors tell funny stories about the antics of the studs. Then the moment of truth arrives and the student's track aircraft is put on the screen.

There are three possibilities--T-38 (fighter, bomber track), T-1(tanker, transport track) or U-H1 (helos). This moment is where some dreams are dashed, some are confirmed (so far) and some come as a complete shock. The realization that UPT can actually be successfully completed is being to dawn on the budding pilots. I haven't seen too many bad reactions to track night but there are stories of students shining their asses in front of God and the world. Not a good career move but, hey we are all adults and you are responsible for your our own actions.

That is pretty much the end of the official functions and the beginning of a great party. For now, T-6 phase is over and Phase III is waiting for you. Most importantly, when you finish track select, your odds of successfully completing flight school just went up. That is worth a drink to celebrate. Also, you will say goodbye to your classmates who are tracked to helos. Their follow-on training is conducted at totally different locations.

Also, this is the time to show some class to your instructor pilots. No matter what your opinion is of your T-6 IPs, take a minute and thank them for training you. They had to sit in the back of the jet and listen on hot mike while you puked your guts out and kept teaching you even after you scared them to death in the flights leading up to solo out. No matter if you liked them or not a sincere acknowledgment of their efforts is a good move.

Keys to success in Phase II:

• Take care of yourself--it is absolutely critical to your success in the T-6; UPT is a marathon and you must solidify good habits that will help you complete the program on time.

• Eat proper meals on a regular schedule. Avoid anything greasy or heavy until you get used to how your body reacts to flying. Hydrate properly, you are sweating your ass off in those jets and being dehydrated literally makes you stupid.

• Develop and keep a regular sleep schedule, this is just as important as studying.

• Ensure you are blowing off steam by hitting your workout program. This will help every aspect of your performance.

• Tap into your support system. Regularly call family and friends to keep in touch with the people that matter. They will support you and boost your spirits when UPT gets sticky.

• Take the opportunities to get away from the base and the Air Force. On the weekends, get away from it all, watch a movie, go do a favorite hobby, or just take a drive--anything to clear your mind is key to keeping the stress from eating at you.

• Take pilot training one day at a time. Don't bother thinking or worrying about what will happen next week, next month or next year. Keep your head down, work hard, and concentrate on winning today. Tomorrow will take care of itself.

• On the weekends, watch some inspirational movies and dial up some flying and combat videos on YouTube. Remind yourself why you are here and the goals you have set for yourself. Although there are some dark days, this is really fun and there are literally hundreds of thousands of people who are jealous of you.

• The most important thing--if you start having problems in Undergraduate Pilot Training--ask for help! Not just your class, instructors, or flight commander! Ask anyone that could help you--a sim instructor, a random IP you happen to know, flight commanders at the Sturon, the Chaplain--anywhere! There are resources all around you just begging to be utilized.

- Keep a set of pilot wings and a model of the airplane you want to fly on your study desk. It always helps to see your dreams on the horizon.

Although Phase II is complete and you have finished the learning the T-6 Texan, flight school is about to start all over again. Welcome to Phase III.

UPT--PHASE III

Phase III

T-38
Scheduled length = 120 training days
Programed flight hours = 96 hours
Academic tests = 5 (T-38 Systems, T-38 Applied Aerodynamics, Instruments, Navigation, Advanced Formation)
Checkrides = 3 (Transition, Instruments, 2-Ship Formation)

T-1
Scheduled length = 120 training days
Programed flight hours = 77 hours
Academic tests = 9 (T-1 Systems, Electrical, Avionics, Hydraulics, Environmental, WX radar, Aerodynamics, Instruments, Enroute Navigation)
Checkrides = 3 (Transition, Navigation, Air Mobility Fundamentals)

Milestones = Assignment night, Final UPT Academic Test, Final UPT Stand Up, Final UPT Checkride--GRADUATION!

More than anything else, Phase III is a warm up for the rest of your aviation career. The instruction and pacing of events is a mirror image of the training you will receive in follow-on aircraft. Just as soon as you start to become comfortable in the T-6, pilot training rips you out of your comfort zone and tosses you back to the starting point in a new aircraft. Make no mistake, you are starting at the very beginning, all over again. In this phase of training, flying the jet becomes more secondary as you are tasked to run mission sorties and formation flights while using all available resources, both internal and external, in order to meet the training objectives. Phase II proved that you can fly a jet, Phase III teaches you to run a mission *while* flying a jet.

Phase II ends and Phase III begins quite literally by the physical movement from the T-6 squadron building over to either the T-38 or T-1 building. Because the class splits for students to accomplish their respective training programs in the different aircraft, schedules become separated as well. Even though you are in the same class as your peers in the other airframe, you won't see them very much until the run-up to graduation.

Although you have learned the basics of aviation, you are not an Air Force pilot yet, so any swagger you may have picked up as the senior class in the T-6 squadron better fall away as you enter the T-38 or T-1 arenas. The weekend after track select is an excellent time to regain a little humility and get your head straight for entry into Phase III. People can, and do, wash out in Phase III, so get your game face on and get ready to attack the program.

In the same vein, in Phase III a *slight* air of mutual respect between you and the instructor pilots will develop, more so than during Phase I or II. You are not an equal by any stretch of the imagination, but expect more training and briefings that begin to prepare you for your follow-on aircraft and operational squadron life. Your instructors know that the odds of you completing pilot training are solidly in your favor now, and there is an excellent chance you both could be stationed together in the future. Your training begins to take on a more collaborative feel, and you need be mature enough identify your own weaknesses and overcome them. The best students realize their own weak areas and work to eliminate them--

not just to try and hide until graduation. Remember, ultimately it is *your* training--take advantage of it!

This emphasis on self-identification of weaknesses and the resources to overcome them is a unique feature in USAF pilot training and a key factor in our production of world-class aviators.

You are not a pilot yet, but you can see the goal in the distance.

Whichever track you take--CAF (Combat Air Forces) or MAF (Mobility Air Forces)-- your first stop in Phase III is back at Aerospace Physiology. New aircraft equals one more day of new life support equipment and Physiology training that mirrors the T-6 instruction. Once again, taking the extra personal time to learn how to properly and quickly strap into and out of your new jet pays excellent dividends. By this time, you know that smooth ground operations mean you receive better instruction, which is a big win in your training program. With the new jets come new oxygen systems to learn, along with fresh egress procedures.

For added fun, the T-38 students take the Fighter Aircrew Conditioning Program (FACP) Assessment, which makes certain you are prepared for the physically punishing G-forces you will experience in the Talon. The FACP is a physical conditioning assessment for fighter aircrew, and is one means of improving G-tolerance and optimizing human performance. The FACP is continuing to evolve and you can expect to see changes to it in the future.

Additionally, your class will have another scheduled stop at Aircrew Flight Equipment. The T-38 students get new harnesses for their jet, while the T-1 students see the last of their helmets at UPT.

T-1 students turn in their G-suit, harness and helmet; your days of oxygen masks are over and you will be issued your very own headset for in-cockpit radio communication.

Because headsets are used in a wide variety of civilian aircraft, I recommend doing some shopping and finding the most comfortable ear/head pads possible. (Pads only, the Air Force mandates you use the issued headset) In the airlift/tanker world it will not be unusual to wear your headset for six to eight hours at a time. If you have hotspots or poorly fitted ear or head pads, it can make wearing the headset a living nightmare. Ask your instructor pilots what padding they use and try them out. Sometimes, the issued headset will have good padding, sometimes not. The key to happiness is finding the best, most comfortable inserts possible and making the changes for yourself. This thought process goes beyond just Phase III and the UPT arena. If you are going to be a professional pilot, get the very best equipment money can buy.

Once you complete these blocks of instruction, your time in Aerospace Physiology is complete (until your next aircraft!), and it is back to the flight line and the final dash to the finish line!

Life in Phase III

No matter which track of training you take, T-1 or T-38, some aspects to pilot training do not change:

- Stand Up emergency procedures--except the T-1 students must master the bizarre phenomena of "dual" Stand Up.

- Bold Face/Ops Limits tests

- Weekly EP quizzes

- Academics

- Formal release

T-38 track vs. T-1 track

THE T-38 TALON

The venerable T-38 Talon is as sexy as a training aircraft can get. Paper-thin wings, responsive to the lightest touch, and a nimble sweetheart all combine to make this airplane perfect platform to teach formation, basic fighter maneuvers and high performance operations. Originally fielded in the early sixties, the T-38 was specifically designed to be a high-performance trainer. In those days the "Century Series" fighters (F-100, F-105, F-102, etc.) filled the inventory and with swept wings, high landing speeds and tricky stall characteristics, the Air Force decided to field the new trainer aircraft with those same attributes. The philosophy revolved around the idea of fielding a trainer that is challenging to land so when assigned to operational fighters with the same characteristics, the new pilot would be more skilled from the start. Airspeed and pitch control are critical in the landing phases of flight because stalling in the final turn is a real concern. Keep the proper speed and pitch and the Talon will behave like a champ. Disrespect those factors, and you can find yourself in a final turn stall and buying the farm.

Outside the traffic pattern, the T-38 is truly in her element. She has plenty of power and being so responsive, it makes the airplane the perfect platform to teach formation flying. Flying in fingertip formation (three foot separation!), rejoins, and trail formation are the order of the day for this airplane. In fact, the T-38 is such an excellent platform it has been used as a frontline fighter aircraft in over a dozen foreign countries. An old joke in the Talon world says that the U.S. Air Force is so shit hot that we train in what other people use as their best fighter.

Although long in the tooth, the T-38, is still an amazing trainer and a kick in the pants to fly. If you are going into the high-performance arena, you will love flying this spirited jet.

Since the time I was an instructor in the T-38 there have been a few improvements in the aircraft, namely the HUD and avionics upgrade.

The HUD (Heads Up Display) is a glass reticle mounted on the glare shield of the front cockpit and presents flight data to the pilot without having to look inside the cockpit, hence the "heads up" reference. Additionally, the HUD does not require the pilot to refocus his vision in order to see outside and read the data.

The avionics upgrade to the T-38 is impressive and integrates the Global Positioning System (GPS) technology into the aircraft. Once assigned to the T-38, you will receive dedicated instruction in all the systems, just like the T-6 instruction.

Myth--Tracking to the T-38 guarantees you a fighter. Fact--Although you may track at T-38, you may not have the skillset to survive in the fighter arena. The T-38 track is "universally assignable," which means you can get any aircraft in the inventory on assignment night.

The entire focus of the T-38 program is to get the student ready to enter the Air Force's fighter/bomber community. To that end, the instruction focuses on:

- Ability to safely operate the T-38--Transition Phase

- Fly in poor weather and aircraft navigation--Instrument Phase

- Learn the basics of formation flying, break ups, rejoins, and leading formations (both 2-ship and 4-ship)--Formation Phase

All the basic elements to this training you have seen before in the Phase

II, so nothing here will be totally new. What is new is the speed of the aircraft and the requirement for you to "think ahead."

Think ahead--term tied very closely to situational awareness, it means the ability to accurately interpret information from a variety of sources (engine instruments, airspeed, HUD data, etc.), formulate a plan of action and implement or modify that plan based on additional information.

TRANSITION BLOCK AND CHECKRIDE

The first thing you will notice on your first takeoff in the T-38 is the literal kick in the pants you receive from the afterburner. Jet fuel is dumped into the engine when you advance the throttles to the afterburner range and the resultant increase of thrust is simply amazing. The next thing you will notice is the lack of turn radius in the jet. Although a beautiful aircraft, those paper-thin wings do not grab a lot of air in a turn so turn radius in both the horizontal and the vertical (loop) plane is pathetic. Therefore, every maneuver, every traffic pattern, and every flight must be planned to the nth degree. The speed of the training sorties increases exponentially--both literally and figuratively. Students have trouble in the T-38 phase if they cannot accelerate their thinking and planning to match the new (high speed) reality.

Additionally, the traffic pattern, and your ability to identify and correct deviations, are critical in the Talon. Due to the swept wing design and the associated high-approach speeds, the T-38 operates close to the stall speed on approach. Add in the delicate balance of a proper final turn and it is easy to see why several jets have stalled and crashed in the final turn. I recommend spending a significant amount of your chairflying time on the traffic pattern and the final turn. Have your classmates quiz you repeatedly and carry a set of flashcards on proper airspeed entries for each maneuver and the entire traffic pattern. You must have all these parameters down cold because the speed of the operation does not permit you to spend more than a heartbeat to accurately recall the information. The key is to accelerate your cross check and watch your airspeed in every phase of flight. Does this seem overly tough or unfair to you? Let me assure you that simple transition work is nothing compared to the day you have to fly your future fighter aircraft safely *and* fight it--all the while with the bad guys trying their best to kill you. You are truly in the big leagues now!

As far as the transition checkride in the T-38 is concerned, pay attention to the universal truths of checkrides previously discussed. The biggest areas of concern during your transition check are;

- Getting slow in the final turn

- Busting out of your area during aerobatics--both horizontally or vertically!

- Going below *bingo* or *joker* fuel. Because the T-38 is extremely fuel limited, tight adherence to fuel planning is an incredibly important part of your sorties.

- Patterns and landings!

Everything you learned in the T-6 must move into high gear in the T-38, especially in the traffic pattern. Transition work is just a warm up to move you on to the Instrument block.

INSTRUMENTS AND INSTRUMENTS CHECKRIDE

The overarching thing you will notice about instrument flying in the T-38 is the aircraft is really not set up to fly instruments very well--adequate, certainly safe, but not very good. I won't harp on this area very much because you will be given plenty of flights, simulators, and instruction for this block of training. Pattern work is really not a concern because you will fly most of your sorties in the back seat under "the bag", which is a black out screen that covers the rear canopy and yes, it sucks being under the bag.

The Instrument checkride is a very straightforward sortie, you depart your home base for an "out and back" mission and fly under the bag to simulate being in the clouds. The regular universal truths of checkrides still apply, but with one big bogie. Be extremely careful with changing altitudes and your flight clearance. A major reason students bust the T-38 instrument checkride is because they miss a level-off altitude, usually by going below the assigned altitude--either in the regular air traffic structure or, more critically, during the approach phase. This is simply a failure to pay attention to your clearances. Confirm with air traffic control if you have any doubt in your mind. Remember, when in doubt, speak plain English! This weakness and lack of attention to detail falls into the decision-making and airmanship arena. Watch your altitude clearances and nail the general knowledge, and you will do fine.

FORMATION AND THE FORMATION CHECKRIDE

Formation flying and the associated expertise required to fly it, is the main focus of the T-38 track of Undergraduate Pilot Training. Two- and 4-ship formation flights dominate the latter parts of the syllabus and your capabilities will be taxed to the limit. Aside from the normal stress of academics and Stand Up, vast amounts of your time will be spent chairflying. In the T-6, there was little concern with fuel planning, the Texan sips gas, but in the T-38, fuel planning is critical to every flight. Chairflying and mission planning in the formation block center on completing all the required elements *within the fuel constraints.* Actually flying the jet becomes almost secondary to the stress of building a plan for a formation sortie, going out to fly that form flight, have the unforeseen happen, and you (or your partner) making changes on the fly--pun intended.

Two-ship formation is simply an extension of the same techniques and procedures you learned in the T-6 but every aspect is accelerated, dramatically! Planning and flexibility become much more important and your situational awareness is fully tested--both as the leader *and as the wingman.* When I was a T-38 instructor pilot, I knew a student was ready to graduate when they could fly as a good formation wingman, having enough situational awareness to spot when their leader was making a mistake--entering a maneuver at the wrong airspeed, about to leave the area, going below bingo fuel, etc. Wingman saves are legal, so just a quick word on the radio can save your wingman from busting the ride!

Just as soon as you begin to master the elements of 2-ship, then you are introduced to 4-ship formation work. Four-ship formation demonstrates to you, in dramatic fashion, that adding two more airplanes to the sortie actually increases the planning and execution headaches x100.

Formation checkride is the culmination of all you have learned in pilot training and a time of anxiety and happiness. Anxiety for yet another checkride to complete and happiness because it will be the last one you have in UPT.

All the checkride techniques and advice I outlined before are still in effect. Don't let your guard down or slack off because you see graduation only a few of weeks away! Now is the time to hammer down and kick ass on your last check. As usual, there is nothing in the formation checkride that you have not seen before. Spend some time chairflying the sortie profile and going over general knowledge with your formation partner the night before.

This is critical information--It was true 25 years ago and it is true today, the dumbest single item students bust in the formation checkride is **traffic patterns and landings!** It sounds stupid and it is--students fly a fantastic formation checkride, complete their profiles and return to the traffic pattern. Despite repeated warnings from their instructor pilots, once the students break up the formation in the traffic pattern, it is as if they think the checkride is over. Next thing that happens, they get slow in the final turn and overshoot the final turn, overshoot the pattern, or just plain fuck up the landing and the IP has to intervene. Time and again this happens, so don't let it happen to you! The checkride is not over until you are sitting in the flight room after de-brief.

Once your formation checkride is complete--just like that, Undergraduate Pilot Training is over for you. Normally, you will fly a few more sorties to ensure you have the proper number of hours to graduate. An old joke amongst instructor pilots is--students don't graduate, their gradebook graduates, so there is a lot of administrative items to do to ensure you are truly complete. It is not unheard of to send a student on a solo flight and tell them to make sure and log a loop--it is all about making the syllabus happy.

The only things left for you are assignment night and graduation. Congratulations, if you made it this far--you earned it!

The T-1 Jayhawk

In the nineties, the Air Force decided to put theory into practice and implemented the Specialized Undergraduate Pilot Training program. The physical manifestation of that plan is the T-1 Jayhawk. The Jayhawk is a twin-engine, swept wing aircraft that is the military version of the Beech 400A business jet. The aircraft is considered medium range and sets an ideal platform to learn the details of advanced navigation, airdrop, and air refueling procedures. The T-1 is a fantastic jet for the job it is assigned to do. Normal configuration has a student in the left seat, instructor pilot in the right and another student in the jump seat, which is located aft of the aircraft's center console. A typical sortie is an out and back training mission where the first student will depart the home station in the left seat and navigate to an out base, while the second student sits in the jump seat--instructor pilot in the right seat for both sorties. When the aircraft is refueled, the students switch positions and it is the second student's turn to fly the aircraft back to the training base.

The T-1 track is designed to teach you how to make mission decisions, accomplish your objectives when situations change, and still fly the jet. Along the way, you get a deep immersion into the bedrock of airlift and tanker operations, Crew Resource Management (CRM).

A fundamental change in the T-1 track of training is its dedicated focus on CRM. The ability to work together as a flight team becomes critical in your follow-on aircraft, and teamwork is the linchpin of Phase III. To pound this philosophy into your brain, all aspects of T-1 instruction now feature elements where you will be working with and supporting other classmates--teamwork is key. The configuration of the T-1 is a physical manifestation of this arrangement. During T-1 sorties, you will sit in the left seat of the aircraft or in the jump seat while your class partner is flying his leg of the training sortie. Additionally, you are introduced to "Dual Stand Up." This is the interesting situation where, instead of facing the Emergency Procedure by yourself, a classmate is called at the same time and you handle the EP *together*. Wingman saves are legal, so your partner can assist during the Stand Up, but also both of you can fail it--just to keep you honest. Although it is true that only one person can be in charge (the aircraft commander) and that the cockpit is not a democracy. Dual Stand Up introduces and galvanizes the bedrock of CRM and the ability (responsibility!) of the co-pilot to speak up as a crewmember, especially in an unsafe situation, even if they are not in charge! *Wingman saves are legal!*

TRANSITION BLOCK AND CHECKRIDE

Take offs and landings in the T-1, honestly, are not that difficult. The area maneuvers are very straightforward, and sometimes students believe because of these factors, the T-1 program is easier than the T-38--major mistake. Although the T-1 may be a bit easier to physically fly than the T-38, the sorties are vastly more difficult to execute, and this is the area where student begin to run into trouble.

Just a word about being a good partner in the T-1. DO NOT TURN INTO A VEGETABLE ON THE JUMPSEAT! Jumpseat saves are legal, so be a good wingman by paying attention, following along the flight step by step, and being "Johnny on the spot" for your partner (getting the atis, looking up frequencies, etc.)

In the T-1 transition block, you must adjust to a new site picture during landing. Along with the new viewpoint of the runway, you will have to rethink touch-and-go landings. Despite in-depth explanation and instruction from the IPs, students try to make super smooth landings in the T-1. That is all well and good, but in doing so, it is common for students to "float" the jet down the runway, trying to get the "squeaker" landing. The problem lies when the student floats the jet so far down the runway that is sails beyond the touch down zone (first 0-2000 feet of the runway)--that is an automatic bust. Put the airplane down in the landing zone and quit worrying about being super smooth! Stable and safe is good enough for pilot training and you do not get extra credit for a squeaker.

Two new sciences T-1 student pilots are introduced to are Take Off and Landing Data (TOLD) and climb performance. In a very brief nutshell, TOLD is the very detailed science that calculates the distances for takeoff and landings in aircraft based on such factors as the engine thrust, weight, runway length, pressure altitude, etc. This information is obviously used in take offs and landings, but also in the touch-and-go phases of flight. Because TOLD was a critical factor in a number of high profile aviation accidents, it is a major emphasis item in the airlift/air refueling community. Let me assure you, this is a very exact and detailed science. You will spend a tremendous amount of time in your checkride discussing the definitions involved in TOLD and climb performance and their applications to flight operations.

The transition checkride in the T-1 carries all the same universal truths that you have already learned as far a check preparation is concerned. Additionally, be able to adapt to curveballs during the flight. If you chairfly an exact profile and are given a different clearance or a navigation aid is down for repair, how will you change the profile and complete the sortie?

Flexibility is the key to airpower

Just so you know--students usually hook transition checkrides for pattern spacing for winds--too wide or narrow--causing an overshooting or undershooting and angled final. Also, they bust the check for trying to force the jet to land in a bad situation--too fast, or not correcting a steep final and they don't call the go-around on themselves. Any of these situations causes the IP to intervene and call the go-around on them due to safety of flight. Clean kill!

A caveat about wingman saves during the transition check. *Technically*, the jumpseater is supposed to keep quiet if their partner forgets something simple, like a "cruise" check. You are only allowed to say something if there is a safety of flight issue. Having said that, no one can say much if you cough or rattle some papers if your partner forgets something during the transition checkride.

NAVIGATION AND THE NAV CHECKRIDE

The navigation block of instruction and the associated checkride is the heart of the T-1 phase. Understand this--the navigation section is the "make or break" part of your training, and that is reflected in the fact that the navigation checkride is the most heavily weighted event in the T-1 track of Phase III. Said another way, how you handle the navigation checkride goes a long way to determine if you complete the program, and, more importantly, what assignment you get. Literally, that C-17 to Hawaii is riding on this segment of training.

Like a good student pilot, you have already learned the basics of instrument flying and have established the basics of mission planning in

Phase II. Navigation takes this basic understanding to an entirely different level. In this arena, you (along with your class "crewmember") will plan missions to accomplish specific objectives. This will normally take the form of out-and back-sorties, where you depart your home base, travel to another airport and fly a specific profile consisting of multiple instrument approaches. These can be complex mission sets that require multiple patterns, differing approaches, civilian aircraft operating in the airport environment, and that old nemesis--bad weather. Through all this, you have to fly your planned profile, make appropriate operational changes as conditions change, and utilize all your assets in the aircraft. Oh yeah, somewhere along the way you have to fly the jet and do touch-and-go landings, safely!

What does this actually look like in plain English? You and your partner (with the IP, of course) depart the home airfield to a nearby civilian airport. You plan to enter the holding pattern and shoot a full GPS approach to the longest runway, complete a touch-and-go landing and return to the radar pattern for the next approach. Of course, Lt Murphy has something to say about this and when arrive at the field, you hear the radios are alive with multiple airplanes already in the pattern. When you check in with the approach controller, you get a wicked curveball--"Duke 02, approach control, too much traffic today to work you. I can give you vectors to final approach for a full stop landing, or you can return to your last assigned frequency. State intentions." Now you have to decide what to do and this juggling act of the mission requirements vs. the variables of aviation is the heart and soul of the navigation block of T-1s.

    After instructing hundreds of students in navigation in both UPT and operationally in the C-5 Galaxy, I can tell you for a fact the number one reason people fail in this block of training is poor mission planning. To be successful, you must mentally walk through every step of the sortie to check and re-check that there are no mission stoppers. One time, a student failed to check if an airfield would be open at arrival time. Weirdly enough, that particular airport was closed because it was a state holiday and the student busted his Nav check bigger than Dallas. This is a textbook example of poor mission planning.

Hunting and eliminating variables that can occur during the flight is the essence of good mission planning. You do this by utilizing all the assets at your disposal--taking your time to go over your sortie plan in detail, backing up your partner by double checking his/her plan, and continually asking yourself "what if" to everything. Once the sortie begins, actively managing the mission becomes critical. Let me assure you, during your flight there will be changes to your profile because of a variety of reasons. Changes are to be expected, what must happen is you utilize all your assets and get the sortie accomplished. Can't get a particular approach because of civilian traffic? Re-shuffle the profile and do it later. Weather starting to deteriorate? Have the jumpseater check the weather at the alternate airport.

You are not cheating, you are utilizing all the assets available to you to make the mission happen--that one sentence is the core of navigation and when you reach that point, you earn the title of "Mission Hacker."

The navigation check is the culmination of all the mission planning and sorties you have done to date. As usual, the check will not contain any element that you have not seen multiple times before. If you are doing something you have never done before--stop! The checkride is set up as a straightforward out-and-back sortie. You will either fly the first leg of the mission and jumpseat on the way back or visa-versa.

As with the T-38 formation checkride, a big percentage of students bust the ride for failures in basic airmanship--turning the wrong way in holding, a poorly-executed circling, or the worst of all, overshooting final on your very last approach back at home station so badly the check pilot has to take the airplane before you join the T-6 runway operation! Just like the T-38, don't fail your checkride because you screw up the traffic pattern and landing. Risk management, decision-making, and situational awareness are all important elements to your sortie, but basic flying the aircraft is still the most important part of your Nav check.

Mission Familiarization and final checkride

Before you know it, the stress and aggravation of the navigation block is behind you and Mission Familiarization begins. Make no mistake, you have not completed pilot training until you walk across the stage and receive your wings. Stay focused and hammer out your last UPT checkride. Remember, the assignment of your dreams might just be a few points away. If you work hard and stay focused, you might be able to finish a little stronger and take that C-130 to Germany from the person ahead of you in class ranking--we call that sweet justice.

Mission familiarization is basic formation and low level flying in the T-1. Both elements are designed to simulate air refueling and airdrop missions, respectively. We won't get too far into the weeds, because these mission sets are complex to explain on paper and have their own unique language that would not be useful to you at this point in your aviation career.

During the simulated air-refueling block of instruction, you (and your student partner) will plan and execute a T-1 formation sortie in the training airspace. Major elements to refueling, both as the "tanker" and "receiver" aircraft are conducting a safe and steady rejoin in the area, followed by formation flight as the "receiver" moves into the air refueling position.

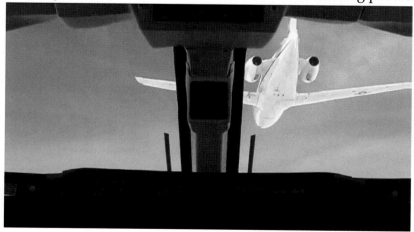

As with all formation--relax! Wiggle you toes and try to put the aircraft into your personal visual cues so that you know you are in exactly the right spot.

The airdrop portion is very straightforward and proper mission planning will make this block of instruction fun. In this phase, you will plan to fly on low-level routes and simulate an airdrop onto a specific target along the training corridor. The U.S. Air Force literally wrote the book on airdrop, and our combat operations during Afghanistan are nothing short of incredible. Having said that, your follow-on aircraft will give you the expertise to drop critically needed supplies on a dime. Airdrop training in the T-1 will give you a frame of reference and a common language. Your next aircraft's schoolhouse will make you an expert.

The Mission Familiarization checkride, is a no-surprises evaluation that measures your ability to run a mission and make proper decisions when changes occur--much like the navigation check. During this checkride you will conduct a simulated refueling mission and a low-level to a simulated airdrop on a target. The major focus on this ride is *not* how fast you can make a re-join or stick the airdrop target, it is your ability to make sound, logical decisions to safely run a mission. In fact, if the weather is bad in the training area or along the low level track, the syllabus permits the entire checkride to be complete if you decide it cannot be accomplished once you are in the air. Of course, you are evaluated on the areas you actual complete on the ride.

Like the T-38 formation checkride, do not fuck up your last checkride in pilot training by screwing up a simple portion of the flight. Once you are recovering the jet back to base, do not let your guard down and bust for something stupid. Do not rely too much on the autopilot. (Yes, there is an autopilot in the T-1 and you are allowed to use it.) It is possible to over-rely on the autopilot and overshoot the final approach. This results in your T-1 formation blundering into the T-6 pattern and causing IP intervention. Ask for simple vectors to final and fly an easy instrument approach to a full stop. You will feel like an idiot (deservedly so) if you float your landing outside of the touchdown zone, so don't.

These are really embarrassing reasons for students to hook because these are incredibly simple and stupid. Don't let this happen to you.

Get your game face on for the mission familiarization checkride and kick ass!

ASSIGNMENT NIGHT!

A huge milestone in your aviation career and the realization of what you have been working towards all these years--assignment night. Your odds of completing flight school are now solidly in your favor, and it is a time for celebration--a small one.

Assignment night is the moment you find out officially what aircraft you will fly after flight school, and it is a major pivot point in your life. You have been dreaming of so many different aircraft for so long, to finally know what you are going to fly as an aviation warrior can swing your emotions wildly.

From the big Air Force's point of view, assignment night is the next step in the factory production and is all part of keeping the pipeline of replacement pilots moving forward. The actual nuts and bolts of how the process works are surprisingly straightforward. Air Force Personnel Center (AFPC) releases a batch of aircraft assignments to the pilot training bases. The flight commanders from the T-1, T-38, T-6 and student squadrons meet and the documentation of your performance over the past 50 weeks is the basis for your rank order on the list. The rank order takes into account everything you have done since zero day--every academic test, flight maneuver, EP quiz, Bold Face/Ops limits, and Stand Up are tossed into a magical gonkculator that spits out a rank order. It is basically the sausage making of a meritocracy. Next, the group begins pairing assignments with what you have listed on your "dream sheet".

Having witnessed the process on a number of occasions, let me tell you how it really works. The group looks at the sheet of assignments and the students. The top performers' assignments are easy: F-22 to the top T-38 student and C-17 to Hickam for the top T-1 student. The next couple of assignments go quickly as well… F-16 to the next T-38 person, and for the next ranking T-1 student who wants to be a FAIP--easy, T-1 to the UPT base. After the first five or six students/assignments, things start to bog down. That is when the assignment group drops to the bottom performers--last T-38 student gets a B-52, last T-1 student gets an E-3 or RC-135 to a remote/cold location. The group works their way *up* the list at this point and this goes pretty easy as well. It is when the group hits the middle four or five students/assignments that it becomes very difficult for everyone. I will say this unequivocally--I have never seen a case where the assignment group did not honestly try to give a student the aircraft what they wanted. Also, I have never seen or heard of the assignment team intentionally screwing over student or giving someone an assignment for political reasons. I defy anyone to show me an example where that supposedly happened.

The assignment priorities go just like this:

- Needs of the Air Force

- Assignment availability

- Student desires

Sometimes, the airplane a student wanted was just not available or the airplane might be available, but another student earned it more. It is at this point where the student's dream sheets are broken out for real and the gut-churning work begins. The mixing and matching is tough, because the desired airplane is not available and you are looking at the rank order list of the student's preferences. I have literally seen the last two assignments get handed out because student A listed one of the two remaining aircraft one spot higher on their dream sheet than student B. Weirdly, in this meritocracy, the last person usually gets their assignment by default rather than by selection.

FAIP'D

Just a quick note about being selected as the backbone of the entire pilot training system--First Assignment Instructor Pilot--FAIP. It may not feel this way at the moment, but being selected as a FAIP is a great deal, and honestly, a huge honor. You are being chosen because of your flying ability, your potential as an instructor pilot, and your professionalism/work ethic. Most importantly, you must have the right personality for the work; nobody wants to hire a douchebag to work with for the next three years. The key to a great FAIP assignment is to dedicate yourself to racking up a ton of hours, completing all the professional military education you can, and earn a master's degree! If you do those three things, you will depart the FAIP assignment far ahead of your peers in regular flying assignments--trust me on this.

My very good friend, Captain Courtney Vidt, sent out this email to her T-1 student class, and with her kind permission, I reprint it here. Courtney does an amazing job capturing the essence of being a FAIP. To set the tone, Capt. Vidt is addressing her student pilots during the time they are rank ordering the aircraft on the "Dream Sheet."

So you want to be a FAIP... or at least you're thinking about maybe putting it in your top 10... or you secretly wonder what it would be like to be a part of the elite group called the Mafia. Well since a good amount of you have mentioned it lately, let's talk about it.

- *To Be Competitive: You should aim to be in the top 1/3 of your class, help out your buddies (we look for team players and the ability to instruct), work hard, have a good attitude and be someone that we as instructors would not mind spending the next 3 years working alongside of.*

- *The Truth of the Situation: You don't choose FAIP, FAIP chooses you. Seriously though, a lot of it comes down to timing. Is there a slot available? Do you fit the above qualifications? Did someone that's ahead of you put it higher on his or her list? Or did you just get lucky and get selected to spend the next 3 years of your life in lovely Enid, Oklahoma?*

• *What happens after you get FAIP'd: We send you to Randolph for the best 4-5 months of your FAIP career (depending on who you talk to). T-1 PIT is just the graduate level of UPT (without the formal release, Stand Ups and EPQs... it's awesome). T-6 is a bit stricter but still a graduate-level course. The academics are the same as the UPT academics you did here, so it's not too bad. You may or may not get to go to SERE and Water Survival (budget depending) or you might have to wait until you drop your follow-on aircraft.*

• *A Few Pros and Cons: You spend the next 3 years of your life in Enid while your classmates go out and travel the world. You make some of the best friends because you work together, hang out together and go on XCs together. You get AC and IP time... as a junior CGO. You still have to compete for your follow-on assignment. You work... a lot. You fly... a lot!*

• *How to make the most out of being FAIP'd, or whatever A/C you go to: Bloom where you're planted. You're going to get jobs in the squadron that you may or, may not like; do your best at them regardless and learn something from them, make them better than how you found them too. Have a good attitude, you can have bad days, but no one likes a Negative Nancy. Be a subject matter expert at your craft, as a FAIP you are the go-to for T-1isms. As a new co-pilot in a MWS aircraft your job is to know the aircraft inside out. Enjoy what you do, you're getting paid to fly... how cool is that!?*

In my opinion, being FAIP'd is the best deal for a brand new pilot, but then again, I am biased because I was one!

Usually, assignment night is held in the base club on a Friday night about two-three weeks prior to graduation, and it is an expanded version of track select. Classes go all out to have a big party and themes for the big event. Lots of food and drinks are the order of the day. It is not unusual to have family, friends, and other pilots come from across the country to enjoy the festivities: it is that big of an event.

Assignment night begins with the class presenting the wing commander with the patch board. The patch board is the giant version of your class patch made into a huge board, suitable for hanging on the wall. At this point, the assignment night video is played to get the crowd excited.

The tension builds as each student is brought before the entire wing. The T-1 and T-38 flight commanders are the emcees for the event and they usually tell funny stories about each student as they come forward. After the laughter, the new assignment aircraft appears on the projection screen and your life changes in a moment. For some, it is the realization of a dream, for others, it can be a disappointment when they see that their performance did not match their ambition.

A note to the Air National Guard and Air Force Reserve sponsored students-- just because you have been "picked up" by a Guard or Reserve unit that flies fighter aircraft does not mean you will automatically go back to that unit to be a pilot. Pilot training instructors have the obligation to uphold the training standards and evaluate whether a student has the skill set to safely operate in the fighter aircraft community. It is possible to go through the T-6 and T-38 training program and __not__ be recommended for fighters. This can come as shock to some Guard/Reserve students when they step forward on assignment night, expecting to be confirmed as an A-10 pilot and getting a C-26 support aircraft instead. A word to the wise-- you are guaranteed nothing in UPT.

Having seen dozens of assignment nights over the years, here are a few observations for you to think about before you step forward to get your aircraft.

- Go easy on alcohol before your assignment. I've seen some drunken idiots do some truly stupid things in front of God and the world on assignment night. You don't want to have to go to the wing commander's office first thing on Monday morning, do you?

- I was there when the guy got FAIP'ed into a T-37 and watched him make a complete ass of himself. When the assignment was announced, his soon-to-be squadron commander stood up from the front row and draped a squadron scarf around his neck and handed him the squadron patches. This ass threw all the stuff on the ground and *stomped on it*, walked away from his new squadron commander without saluting, and walked out of the room while his wife was in tears. Needless to say he killed his reputation in a one-minute (alcohol-fueled) temper tantrum. I know for a fact the FAIPs and regular instructor pilots made his life hell for the next year solid and he got a crappy follow-on assignment. Bottom line--have a little class, even if you are unhappy with your assignment. After all, you earned it by your performance.

• If your classmates get something they did not want (drone), take good care of them. Buy them drinks all night, look for the positive and be a good dude/dudette to them. The golden rule applies here and they will appreciate the consideration.

Make no mistake, getting the actual assignment is a shock. You might be elated, dejected, or even pissed, but usually you will just be surprised. "Not exactly what you hoped for, but an exciting airplane/mission" is a common statement I hear in the week after assignment night. If you are pissed, you have permission to be mad over the weekend, then get over it and get back to work. Chances are, there are pilots in your squadron that just came from that assignment, go find them and get the real information on your future. **Do not** mope around and be pissed off--first off, you are not done with pilot training and students have washed out of pilot training *on graduation day--I have personally witnessed it!* Secondly, even a flying assignment you were not looking for is infinitely better that working in a cube farm under florescent lights. My brother's quote really applies here--"I would cut your throat to change places with you, so don't complain."

GRADUATION

Miracles of miracles, you wake up one day and realize that it is all over--finally! All the years of work, worry, and stress is about to pay off. You have made it and set yourself on a path of an amazing career and life. The graduation ceremony itself runs smoothly, because each Undergraduate Pilot Training base puts one on every three weeks. Usually held on Friday, graduation consists of the graduation ceremony itself and graduation dinner that evening. Additionally, there are usually "red carpet" simulators and static display aircraft made available for family and friends--take advantage of them!

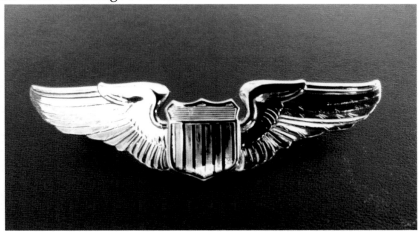

In many ways, graduating from UPT is more significant milestone than graduating from college, because getting your wings sends you into your chosen profession.

Just a few things to remember about UPT graduation:

• DO NOT lose focus on flight training! Until the last checkride and flight are complete, you HAVE NOT finished UPT. I personally have witnessed a student wash out of flight school on the morning of graduation. It is horrible for everyone involved. Keep your game face on until all your training events are complete. It is not over until it is over.

• If you followed my initial advice--dry-cleaned and stored your service dress uniform under a plastic sleeve--you are good to go. If you didn't listen, get your uniform up to speed early. If you wait to the last minute, Murphy has an open invitation and you could be scrambling at the last second to get a proper uniform together.

• During the graduation events, take the opportunity and enjoy the moment. What you have accomplished is staggering in its scale, and it is a truly a nexus in the trajectory of your life. This is a busy, stressful time (completing last flights, family coming into town, packing to move, etc.), and it is easy to let the moment pass in a blur. Take the time to enjoy the people who come to celebrate with you, thank those who helped you achieve your dream, and reflect on the road you have travelled, because when you wake up on the Monday after graduation, it starts all over again in a new location and new aircraft.

• In the days after UPT, you will be offered the opportunity to take the Federal Aviation Administration's Commercial Instrument type rating test. TAKE AND PASS THIS TEST! The rating lasts a lifetime and it is the only time the FAA acknowledges the hard work it takes to become an Air Force pilot. Even if you plan to retire as a four star general--take the test. You never know where life will take you. It is pretty easy.

One final note about UPT and your class: in all likelihood, the graduation dinner is probably the last time you will ever be together again as a class. After being thrown together for a tumultuous year with the highest highs and the lowest lows, it all ends incredibly quickly. Some of your classmates will leave for their next training assignments literally the Monday morning after graduation. Within weeks most everyone is scattered to the four winds and will not ever all be in the same place at the same time again, which is the nature of military service. However, it is the nature of Air Force flying that you will run across each other all over the world in completely unexpected places. Walking out of a bar in Hawaii, in a flight line bunker during a mortar attack in Balad, Iraq, and the flight planning room in Spangdalem, Germany, are all places I have run into guys from my class--Air Force aviation is just that random.

Just like that, Specialized Undergraduate Pilot training is complete. Years of effort all come together and now you have become a fully rated pilot for the United States Air Force. The nation has invested a tremendous amount of money and time in your training (around $1,000,000!) and now it is time to start repaying that debt. As usual, once you begin feeling comfortable in one environment, it is time to head to your next challenge-- the Flying Training Unit and your operational aircraft.

WHAT COMES NEXT?

FORMAL TRAINING UNIT

After all the drama and excitement (and stress) of Undergraduate Flying Training, earning your silver wings and being a fully rated pilot can be a bit of a mental dip. Don't get me wrong, waking up every morning and knowing the pressure of UPT is over is glorious. But, you have been working so hard and sacrificed so much of your life to pursue this objective that when you achieve that goal, the next day can be a little confusing. Basically, your brain is saying to you, "now what?" This chapter will take you from UPT graduation through the first 18-24 months of your first duty base and the first downrange deployment.

Once you graduate from pilot training, your focus changes from earning your wings to being ready to fly your follow-on aircraft, and that is called mission qualified (mission qual). Your primary goal now is to become fully mission qualified as quickly as you can in your new aircraft.

After Undergraduate Pilot Training graduation, there can be a lull of a few months before you actually depart to your first operational squadron. The training pipeline can be fickle, so be prepared to stay at your UPT base until your Formal Training Unit (FTU) class--anywhere from one day to six months is possible. Some of your classmates will depart on the Monday morning after the Friday graduation, and to be honest, you will probably not see most of your classmates all together again. The important thing to remember is that your reputation has started in UPT, but now that you are entering the pipeline of your community (C-17, F-16, U-28) it becomes incredibly important. Are you a good dude/dudette or are you a dirt bag? Now continues the foundation towards answering that question.

The Air Force is large overall, but the individual aircraft communities are pretty small, so once you get to your FTU, the reputation you make for yourself will precede you to your first squadron. When I was a squadron commander, I had my deputy call the instructors at the C-5 training school house and find out about the new pilots who were inbound to my squadron. I guarantee your new commander will do the same. The words I wanted to hear about my new pilots were--hard working, dedicated, good stick, great attitude. Get the picture?

The formal training units are extensions of pilot training, so show up on day one with your game face on. Your class will typically be much smaller than pilot training--usually five to eight pilots is pretty common, and you will begin to learn the business of your new aircraft.

First, there is a sea change in the entire philosophy of your training going forward. You are still in student mode, but because you have earned your pilot wings, the instructors are focused on your success. Look at it from the instructor's point of view: one day, they literally may place their lives in your hands, because you are in their aircraft community and going to war with you is a real possibility. The focus of FTU is to teach you how to fly your aircraft and then how to employ it as a weapon of war.

My advice is to hit the ground running at your FTU. Roll back into UPT mode and hammer down the Bold Face/Ops Limits from day one. Follow up with a deep dive into chapter Three of the Dash-1 with special focus on the notes, warnings, and cautions, and you will be golden--no matter your aircraft. All those rules of thumb you learned about checkrides will be valid in FTU, so you should knock the program out of the park.

Pilots occasionally wash out of their follow-on schools, so keep in the books and ask for help if you start getting behind. You know the drill from your UPT days, and remember, the schoolhouse and your instructors want you to succeed.

> *If you are going to an airlift, tanker, or bomber aircraft, I <u>highly recommend</u> you become a stone-cold expert in all things related to take off and landing data and climb performance. It is an Air Force level emphasis item, so you will have the fine details of the science of TOLD pounded into your nugget. Save yourself a lot of heartache and become an expert in TOLD.*

Once you finish FTU and arrive at your first base, things can seem overwhelming. Too many things to do and you want to start flying right away. Take it from me, relax and spend the quality time now to get your "house" in order. This basically means to take the time to find a good place to live. I won't talk about lifestyle, just smart choices. If you are single and move into a hip apartment complex with plenty of hot members of the opposite sex, that might be cool part of the time, but are the midnight pool parties going to keep you awake when you have an 0530 takeoff time? If you are married--is the cute rental house in the "transitioning" neighborhood really a good deal if your wife gets frightened by the homeless guy that lives in the ally out back and pees on your garage each morning? A little extra time and effort here will save you some headaches and the ultimate bogie of having to take leave from work just so you can move to a better location at a later date. It will pay big dividends later, I promise.

When you check into the squadron's administrative section, they will hand you several pages of inprocessing checklists. These can be tedious and painful exercises in frustration--think "Closed for training" at a lot of different offices you visit. Even if the base runs a "newcomers' flight," you will have to travel from location to location all over the base to get briefings, fill out forms and provide information. Generally, your flying squadron does not even want to see you before the in-processing checklists are complete. Although this seems never ending and tiresome, put in the extra effort to finish these ASAP. Basically, you are on your own time to complete these checklists. Instead of calling it a day at 1530 hours and driving home, like everyone else, keep pressing the system and see if you can get just one more item finished, each day. Those lists are standing between you and flying, so attack them! By chipping away at the inprocessing checklists a little more each day than the next pilot, you will complete them faster and get on the flying schedule that much quicker. The quicker you get on the flying schedule, the quicker you will become mission qualified (MQ), and that ultimately the reason you are there.

Once the in-processing checklists are complete, the scheduler will at least look at you. Your flying career can start in earnest.

ADDITIONAL DUTIES

An unpleasant part of being an Air Force pilot are the dreaded "additional duties." These tasks are the various jobs that have to be done to keep the wheels of the squadron, operations group and wing rolling. Basically, pilots are assigned jobs in the squadron or loaned out to different organizations to accomplish the required work that keeps the military bureaucracy moving. I know it is not fair, but the bureaucratic work has to be done. Just consider it the price you pay for permission to fly the finest aircraft in the world. Having said that, if you maneuver to avoid getting an additional duty or do a crappy job in the work, you are dumping on someone else who has to do extra duty to cover for your sorry ass. This "buddy fucker" behavior kills your reputation.

If you happen to get an additional duty you personally enjoy, that is great, but remember, you are an Air Force pilot, not a career "additional duty" officer. I remember one general officer who lectured me on how he became a general. He told me that when he was named snack bar officer (snacko) in his first squadron, he dedicated himself to being the "best snacko in the Air Force" and that is why he was so successful. He told me that he focused all his effort and talent on his additional duties, and that got him promoted early. Good thing that worked out for him, because I can tell you for a fact that he might have been the Air Force's best snacko, but he royally sucked as a pilot. Your profession is flying, not filling the drink machine. It sounds simple but some pilots will confuse the two jobs, pilot and additional duty, and spend all their time and effort on their additional duty. I have always used the one-hour per day rule of thumb for additional duties, and that seems to work well. Basically, I plan to spend an hour per day on my additional duty. Sometimes that is an hour a day or five hours on just one day--as an average. That is usually plenty of time to accomplish 90% of the work that needs to be done.

PROFESSIONAL PILOT

You made it to the ranks of the professional Air Force pilot! Now you get to enjoy some of the perks of the job, namely your pro (professional) gear. Sunglasses, wristwatches, travel bags, and boots are just a few of the goodies you get to indulge in. As an Air Force officer and pilot, you do not wear designer ties or custom suits. No one will give you an expensive leather briefcase for the office. Put some of your resources (money) into the things you will use professionally every day. I am a firm believer that if you use a tool or implement every day, professionally, it should be of such quality that when you pick it up, your brain automatically says, "Oh yeah, this is awesome." Okay, now that I gave you permission, make sure that you spend your money wisely and get some good stuff. Before plunking down your hard earn cash on that cool Brietling watch ($3,500), make sure it will suit your needs for years to come. Ask around your FTU and squadron to see the very best gear that other pilots are using. Also, ask around to see if someone is making a bulk buy or if you can get a special discount on a particular item because of a military association with a high-end product. Don't confuse expensive for the best quality! Make sure you get the very best comfort and quality that will last you for years to come.

THE LAUTENBERG AMENDMENT AND DOMESTIC BLISS

This is a major bogie and something for you to watch out for every day of your professional life. Screw this up and you have fucked your career up, big time.

The Lautenberg Amendment is an amendment to the Gun Control Act of 1968 and President Clinton signed it into law in 1996. The law makes it a felony for those convicted of misdemeanor crimes of domestic violence to ship, transport, possess, or receive firearms or ammunition. This means that military members that are convicted for domestic violence cannot carry weapons, period.

So, assuming you have a misunderstanding with your bf/gf and get a domestic violence conviction—well, then my friend, you are in quite a pickle. The bottom line is that if you are convicted of domestic violence, you are useless as a pilot. As your commander, what can I do with you? All people deployed downrange must be current and qualified on their respective firearms. For Air Force pilots, that means the M9 Beretta pistol. The first item on the agenda of M9 training is to check and make sure no one is ineligible for the class because of a Lautenberg Amendment conviction--and it is checked. Frankly, as a responsible squadron commander, I am going to put my resources--sorties, training classes, and schools slots on pilots that help the squadron prepare for downrange. If you have a domestic violence conviction, you no longer fill the bill. In a word, your career is effectively over.

Weirdly, as interpreted by the Department of Defense, the prohibitions do not preclude an airman from operating major weapons systems and crew-served weapons, such as tanks, missiles and airplanes.

The takeaway from all this is to think ahead and never lose your cool with your significant other. Think ahead by being very careful in your choices in a partner. Nobody gets married thinking they will get a divorce, but you can save yourself a world of problems and money by doing two things.

1. Be very discerning of whom you begin a relationship with. I understand being young and that passions run hot in your demographic. Think seriously if the person you are in love with will be suitable to this life. Lots of moves, young children in austere locations, and you being gone frequently to schools and deployments are terrible burdens on the best of relationships.

2. Make sure your significant other knows what he or she is signing up for before commitments are made. An honest explanation of the lifestyle will do more to save you future headaches than virtually anything else you can do. The Air Force has many resources available so your intended knows if he or she wants this life. Remember, no matter how it works out--you volunteered to lay your life on the line, your partner didn't join up with you and their crime is simply loving you. For that, your significant other deserves all the information necessary to make informed decisions.

Finally, no matter what, keep your cool and walk away. I know that blood runs hot and passions can be overwhelming, but you have to stay in control of yourself. Mastering your passion means walking away when arguments could possibly turn physical. The second it does, you have failed and literally pissed your career away. Never, ever lay a hand on your significant other, and you have nothing to be worried about.

GET READY TO DEPLOY

Once you have become mission qualified on your particular aircraft, the countdown timer begins towards your deployment, which normally is about 18-24 months after arriving on station. The following steps will make your preparations easy.

• Get a pre-deployment checklist--there will be plenty just laying around or ask the pilot section for one.

• Start collecting the items on the checklist because it will save you a ton of headaches later. For example, if you are required to have 12 pairs of socks before you leave, when will most people get those socks? The day before departure date, and I guarantee the stores will be out of what you need. Wouldn't you rather spend those last days before leaving enjoying your family, rather than driving all over creation trying to get ready to travel?

- Plan ahead and get your financial house in order. While you are gone, how are you going to manage your affairs? Does your wife have all the account information she needs? What do you want your father to do with your car while you are gone?

Let me tell you for an absolute fact--you cannot run a household from downrange. I have seen plenty of people try and every single one of them failed. Also, do not plan on having Internet, email or cell phones available to you while deployed. I know you think you are going to a location that is fully connected electronically, but orders can and do change overnight, so you have to be prepared for the worst-case scenario. Think of yourself as a corporation--how will you run the business of *you* with the CEO out of the country?

PHYSICAL FITNESS

Are you physically ready to deploy? As we discussed before, the Air Force requirement for your physical fitness is only to pass the fitness assessment. Having said that, are you ready to go to war--physically? Honestly, in the ultimate test of warfare, passing the fitness assessment is not good enough.

What level of fitness do you need? That's a good question and one I can't answer for you.

In my opinion, the United States' capability in combat search and rescue (CSAR) has gone down over the years, mainly because we have not had to use it very often. On real-world combat missions, I have been briefed that if my aircraft were shot down, I would need to walk 30+ miles-- through enemy territory--just to get to a spot where CSAR could come and get me. Can you walk 50 miles, right now, today? How about if I put a few hundred bad guys between you and safety, hunting for you?

The bottom line is that your level of fitness above the fitness assessment is up to you, but if the chips are down, can you complete the mission and save yourself?

Extra gun practice and hand-to-hand combat training

The Air Force is not going to give you enough training with your issued handgun. The level of training you get is just enough so that you are safe carrying the gun, but that is it. Because of this, you may consider purchasing your own weapon and getting some additional trigger time. I suggest buying the civilian version of the issued weapon (M9 = Beretta 92FS) and get as much realistic training you can get. If the Air Force goes to no-shit, people-are-dying war tomorrow, will you have the time or opportunity to get any training on your own? The short answer is "no."

Some people may laugh, but give some serious thought to getting realistic hand-to-hand combat training. Brazilian jiu-jitsu, mixed marital arts, and boxing are all possible areas that are worth your time. Aside from the increased physical fitness, you might need the skills one day and the required muscle memory takes practice.

Honestly, it is ludicrous the lack of combat training you receive. There may be some eye rolling or laughing when you reveal that you do this additional training but I am sure Lt Moaz al-Kasabeh would beg to differ. You do remember Lt al-Kasabeh, don't you? He was the Jordanian F-16 pilot that was shot down by ISIS and burned alive in a cage. If you need a refresher, go on YouTube and remind yourself of the horror.

How to rise quickly

After 25+ years in the flying arena and working in virtually every office in a modern flying squadron, I have developed a laundry list to help you rise to the top of the squadron.

Master your aircraft. It seems a little basic, but you must become an expert in your weapon system. It is not sufficient to study enough just to pass a test or checkride. You are going to take your aircraft to war and you must understand *why* the individual systems work the way they do. This learning should take whatever form works best for you--go down to maintenance, visit the factory to see how the jet is made, or just read "the books" until you are an expert—these are all ways to gain the mastery. However, you never know enough or all there is to know.

Make a handshake agreement with the scheduler. The pilot schedulers have a difficult job. Aside from filling the daily flight schedule, they have to fill a variety requests all day long. Every day, organizations call the squadron and ask for a pilot/officer to fill a tasking (for example a pilot to serve as a static display officer--stand beside your aircraft and answer questions while the local rotary club visits). The schedulers then have to juggle their normal duties and track down people to fill these taskings. As you know, pilots are smart and duck the scheduler's calls.

Do yourself a favor, make a handshake agreement with the schedulers to the effect of, "Look, I know you have crappy taskings you have to fill every day. If you have problems filling any tasking, call me and I will do it, no bitching, no complaining. All I ask is that you take care of me on the backend." When the schedulers love you, you have a wonderful pilot life-- good deals, early schools and extra time off are all benefits you can expect.

Become a Subject Matter Expert (SME)--Once you get a solid grasp on your aircraft, it is time to branch out your knowledge and work to become a subject matter expert in some aspect of your mission. There will be some subject or aspect about your aircraft or mission that you think is really cool. It can be anything that you enjoy learning about. You want to pick an arena and become the hands-down expert in it. Maybe it is airdrop in the C-130, employing the 20mm cannon on ground targets in the F-16, or C-5 combat tactics--open your brain and look for outside channels to expand your knowledge. Would you take a day of leave to go speak to an authority on the subject? If the answer is "yes" you are on the right track.

Use every opportunity to learn the subject and *teach* it to your squadron! Pretty soon, the wing will know that you are the "go to" person when that topic is being discussed and that is a very good thing. Subject matter experts rise quickly, are tasked in special missions and are given incredible access and opportunities.

Help the cause--My rule of thumb is the golden rule plus 10%. Do the little things that help the "work" of the squadron get done. For better or worse, the Air Force operates as a bureaucracy, and your squadron has to feed the machine. Even though you may not be tagged with a specific additional duty, volunteer to help out the schedulers and executive officers. They have a ton of tasks to complete on a daily basis, and even running a quick errand is a Godsend.

Absolutely volunteer to assist with anything the deployed members may need. Sometimes it is mowing a yard or giving a ride to the airport--these small tasks are critical to the deployed families and the lifeblood of our brother/sister hood.

Finally, be a great dude/dudette--paying it forward is the watchword. For example, if you are single, volunteer to sit the operations desk on Christmas Day so the married people can have time at home with their families. For the married folks, volunteer to work on New Year's Eve so the single people can go out.

If you can give just a little bit more than you get, you will have a great squadron.

So there it is! After graduating from Undergraduate Pilot Training, there is no manual or guidance on how to arrive and thrive at your first flying squadron. The information I have revealed to you is exactly what I wish I had when I arrived at my first squadron so many years ago. I have kept the information in this chapter generic so it does not matter what airframe you are going to--the tips and good ideas are universal. As always, hit the ground running, work hard and be a good wingman, and you will be just fine.

CONCLUSION

Becoming an Air Force pilot has been an incredible career and life for me. I started this book out asking you a pretty simple question--do you want this life? I had to answer this very question for myself a long time ago and the answer was yes. Looking back over the 27 years since I entered pilot training, I can honestly say that there was never a time I regretted my commitment to becoming a pilot or choosing this life for a career path. Being an Air Force pilot has allowed me to fly around the world and see the United States from a totally different point of view. I have experienced cultures and met amazing people, which would have been impossible if I chose a pedestrian career path. Best of all, seeing the world via a cockpit has galvanized my faith in American exceptionalism and why the United States is still the beacon of hope for the world to follow. America is surely not perfect, but we acknowledge our shortcomings and work to lift up all mankind. Flying the world has given me that priceless perspective. Further, no matter how hard my chosen path became, the opportunity to move airplanes for a living has always (and still is) fantastic. My missions into combat were the culmination of years of work, and I have nothing but pride for the opportunity to serve the country that has given me so much. Best of all, I have made lifelong friends who have shared the best and worst of times together. Shakespeare had it right when he wrote, "We few, we happy few, we band of brothers..." In the final calculation, I truly feel sorry for the people who have to grind out a living in the regular nine-to-five world.

Just getting to Specialized Undergraduate Pilot Training is a long, hard road. Aside from the hurdles the Air Force puts in front of you, there are the people in your life who tell you that it is impossible for you to become a pilot or that you don't meet the physical/intelligence standards. While these friends and family members mean well, they are poison and plant the seeds of doubt in your mind. You have heard me say repeatedly through this book, self-doubt is why the vast majority of people never live the lives they want or reach their goals. I can say unequivocally that ignoring the "nay-sayers" and achieving my dream of being an Air Force pilot has been worth it every single day.

None of this will happen without commitment and dogged determination from *you*. The trait you have to identify and develop in yourself is tenacity. Even if you choose a different path in life, tenacity will serve you well in achieving all that is possible. Nobody can want it for you, and no one can do the work of pilot training--before, during or after.

If I had it all to do over again, here is what I wish I knew before starting on my journey to the silver wings:

1. The college degree is a means to an end, complete it as quickly and painlessly as possible. Seriously consider an online degree because you can control the pace and timing of your graduation. The quicker you are done, the quicker you are in UPT.

2. Pick the commissioning source that fits your mindset and lifestyle. It would have been a huge mistake for me to attend the Air Force Academy, but ROTC fit me like a glove.

3. Show up at pilot training with all the garbage cleaned out of your life. Settle relationships, finances, and all the drama that can possibly get in your way.

4. The first day at your UPT base, establish a rock-solid baseline of exercise, eating, and sleeping that will set you up for success over the long term. Pilot training will force you to do, so it is much less painful if you do it yourself.

5. Gather all the intel and study aids when you arrive on base. Ask everyone and anyone for their gouge on UPT. Information is the coin of the realm, and it helps remove the mystery of pilot training--gather everything that is out there.

6. Stay in the UOQs the entire time you are in pilot training--the extra money you save having an apartment with your buds is not worth the commute time.

7. Stay single while in UPT, and if relationships start getting sticky, kick them to the curb. Relationships are like buses, there is always another one coming around the corner in a few minutes.

8. Build yourself a kick-ass Paper Tiger for chairflying, complete with control stick--let your imagination run wild.

9. Write this on your mirror in your Q room so you will be reminded of it every day--"Attitude is Everything!" Better yet, tattoo it across your forehead.

10. Work extra hard to get along with every person in your class. You are stuck with them for a year and will have to rely on them during that time. Your goal should be to graduate from UPT without any of them ever knowing that you hate their guts.

11. Ask for help!

12. Know your Boldface Ops/Limits cold a week before starting on the flight line.

13. If someone in the class is struggling in a certain area, help them! Even though you are competing with/against them for class ranking and assignments, one day it will be you struggling in another area and you will appreciate the help.

14. Do more than your fair share to help the class complete the daily, weekly, monthly requirements of flight school. You don't have to do everything, but by doing extra, you will build up a lot of good will amongst the class and IPs.

15. From day one, tell your IPs and classmates the aircraft you want to fly. Keep a model of it on your study desk, along with a set of pilot wings. Physically seeing your goal daily is a powerful motivator--consciously and subconsciously.

16. Be conservative during your checkrides. If the pattern does not look good, go around! The check pilot will be more impressed that you made a safe decision than if you "saved" an awful final turn.

17. Stay in your training area.

18. Go home on holidays.

19. Call family and friends often to keep up your emotional health.

20. If you bust a ride or check, you have two hours to feel sorry for yourself, then shake it off and get back to work.

21. Never give up.

22. Wingman "saves" are legal.

23. Have fun.

24. When you graduate, take the time to thank everyone who had a hand in putting wings on your chest--from that teacher that got you through a tough subject in high school to the life support lady that helped you with the leaky O2 mask. The more people you seek out and thank, the more class and character you have.

That, as they say, is that. I have given you everything I wish I had known before I started on my own journey to the silver wings, some 35+ years ago. I have tried to lay out the road to get you to and through Undergraduate Pilot Training with as many hints and ideas I could throw in along the way.

Being an Air Force pilot is the greatest honor and privilege in my life and one I hope to share with you. It is an amazing journey, and if you have the tenacity, you can make it too.

My last advice is very simple--train like you will go to war tomorrow, love your family and friends fiercely, and enjoy every minute of the journey--it will be over before you know it.

I began this book by asking you a simple question--do you want this life? The answer is--HELL YES!

Check six!

See you on the flight line!

ACRONYMS AND TERMS

- **88 Ride, Progress Checkride** – A checkride that is given to a student to determine if they should continue in normal training or be recommended for elimination check/ 89 Ride.

- **89 Ride, Elimination Checkride** – Checkride given to determine if a student is placed back in to the regular training flow or recommended for elimination from training.

- **AETC** – Air Education and Training Command

- **Air Force Officer's Qualifying Test (AFOQT)** – Standardized test, very similar to the SAT and ACT in design but with more subsections and areas specifically for pilots and navigators. Things to remember about the AFOQT:

- You must complete all the test sections. Even if you are going to be a pilot, you have to complete the navigator section.

- The AFOQT can only be completed twice – make it count!

- You must wait six months between tests.

- Guessing does not hurt your score!

- The most recent score counts.

- The AFOQT score never expire.

- **ALO** – Academy Liaison Officer (Air Force Academy)

- **Assignment Night (Drop Night)** – Event approximately two to three weeks prior to graduation where the student pilots are awarded their follow-on aircraft. Usually a big party conducted at the base's club.

- **ATIS** – Automatic Terminal Information Service, continually broadcast aeronautical data about an airfield. Contains temperature, pressure altitude, and current weather conditions.

- **Bingo Fuel** – Prebriefed amount of fuel that, when reached, the aircraft can return to the airfield (or alternate), using normal recovery parameters and arrive with normal landing fuel. Bingo fuel means it is time to go home and land. You do not go below bingo fuel, period

- **Boneyard** – Aircraft storage facility at Davis-Monthan Air Force Base in Tucson, Arizona. Incredibly cool to see acres and acres of decommissioned aircraft stored in the desert. If you ever get a chance, go there. It will be a highlight of your aviation career.

- **Buy the farm** – Die in an aviation accident. "He stalled in the final turn and bought the farm."

- **CAP – Commander's Awareness Program** – Classification where a student pilot is having trouble in training is identified. This is not necessarily a negative and ensures proper schedule priority, attention, and continuity.

- **Century Series Fighters** – F-100, F-101, F-102, F-105 – Family of fighter aircraft characterized by thin, swept wings, causing fast approach speeds and tricky handling charictieristics at low airspeeds.

- **Chairflying** – Visualization training whereby you imagine you are in a specific situation and go through the routine steps and procedures involved in flying.

- **Clearing turns** – Gentle turns made back and forth on a (mostly) vertical plain that allows the pilot to increase his/her field of vision. Also, it is just a fun maneuver.

- **Clear on the radio** – Process whereby you listen and determine where and in what stage of flight other aircraft are operating, while you are flying. Due to poor Air Traffic Control and radar coverage in much of the world, this skill will keep you alive in the most austere corners of the globe.

- **Climb Performance** – Calculated data that determines the rate of climb of a particular aircraft on a given day. This data is determined from the beginning of the take off roll through the level off altitude and is *critical* to the safe operation of all aircraft.

- **Crew/Cockpit Resource Management, CRM** – Cockpit management system that seeks to use all resources to maintain situational awareness and flight safety. Highly focuses on interpersonal skills between crewmembers.

- **Crosscheck** – The eye/head movement where a pilot checks the various flight instruments during a sortie. By crosschecking properly a pilot ensures stable flight by seeing and mitigating changes in airspeed, altitude and heading before they become critically out of acceptable parameter.

- **CSAR – Combat Search and Rescue** – Like the name implies, forces that will come and rescue you in the event you are shot down in combat action.

- **DNIF** – Duty Not Involved in Flying - This is the status the flight surgeon puts you in while you are sick or injured. Do not fly if you are in this physical status! Sounds simple but students screw this up every class. DNIF is not a gauge on how you feel, it is a duty status. If you are DNIF, you cannot fly until you are removed from DNIF status, period.

- **Dollar Ride** – Your first flight in a new aircraft and you are expected to give a dollar to the instructor pilot that takes you up for the first time. This tradition is as old as aviation itself.

- **Dual Stand Up** – Normal emergency procedure testing drill but with the addition of a second student.

- **Failure to progress** – A bad term to be associated with you in UPT. It means that you are not learning at a pace so as to complete the program on the proper timeline.

- **FAIP** – First Assignment Instructor Pilot – Instructor pilots that have completed flight school and have been especially selected to remain at flight school and teach in a specific airframe. FAIP's are the backbone of UPT instruction and fly the vast majority of student sorties. After assignment as a FAIP, the pilots are the Air Force's gold standard of aviation knowledge and excel in their follow-on aircraft. Additionally, FAIP's wrack up a crazy amount of flying hours during their time at flight school.

- **Fighter Aircrew Conditioning Program (FACP)** – Fitness program designed to improve the G-tolerance, G-endurance, and overall cockpit strength and conditioning of aircrews; identify and correct insufficiently conditioned aircrews prior to entering the high-G environment; and establish effective physical conditioning habit patterns.

• **Final Turn** – The 180 degree maneuver in the standard Air Force traffic pattern that takes the aircraft from 1500 feet above the ground to the runway. This descending turn keeps the aircraft close to the runway and maximizes airfield operations. Don't get slow in the final turn!

• **Fingertip Formation** – Standardized formation flown by training and fighter aircraft, can be in both two and four-ship flights. Characterized by the wingman (wingmen) flying in close proximity to lead aircraft – 3 foot separation in the T-38.

• **Fitness Assessment, FA** – The USAF fitness assessment or Physical Training test.

• **Flatliner** – Student that does not progress, does not learn a maneuver or procedure after repeated demonstration. No spark/ aptitude for aviation.

• **Flesh peddlers** – Another name for Air Force Personnel Center. Located as Randolph Air Force base, this organization "drops" the aircraft to your UPT class.

• **Flight Room** – Individually divided rooms in the squadron where the instructor pilots and students have their work/learning space. Usually organized so that each instructor is paired with two students. During UPT students will spend most of their time in this room.

• **Flight Suit (The Bag)** – The utility uniform for Air Force, Navy and Marine Corps pilots. Made of Nomex, the full body suit is fire resistant and has the distinctive addition of multiple pockets, ideally suited for aviation.

• **Floating the jet** – Occurs during landing phase - holding the aircraft off the ground in the flair in an effort to make a soft, smooth landing. Extended time in the flair causes the aircraft to "float" beyond the touchdown zone. Can cause a "long" landing and/or possibly run off the end of the runway.

- **Formal release** – Flight line restriction whereby your class is not allowed to leave the flying squadron unless you are going to an approved location. This is meant to give you time to study and focus your efforts in the aviation arena.

- **Friday T-shirt, Morale Shirt** – T-shirt worn under the flight suit of Fridays that is usually in the squadron colors. Pilots that fail to wear their Friday T-shirts can be "fined" for the mistake.

- **G-Suit** – More properly, the anti-g suit. Chaps like clothing worn over the flight suit that covers the abdomen and legs of the pilot. Interior air bladders expand during increased G maneuvers, preventing blood from pooling in the lower extremities.

- **Global Positioning System (GPS)** – Satellite based navigation system that provides incredibly accurate positioning virtually anywhere on the globe. Air Force pilot training aircraft now have this capability installed and navigation is vastly simplified. Be forewarned; on Day 1 of World War III, our opponent will take down the GPS system. You must always ask yourself, can I fly without GPS today?

- **Ground pounder** – Non-pilot, non-flyer.

-

- **Go** – Two possible meanings. 1) A flying period during the duty day with multiple takeoffs. 2) Shortened slang for a go around.

- **Go Around** – To abandon an approach and/or landing, increase airspeed and altitude and return to the traffic pattern.

• **Gonkulator** – Mythical computer that calculates any/all weird and little understood rankings and lists in the Air Force. This never seen machine calculates anything you do not understand.

• **Gouge** – Information, data, and intelligence on the various aspects of UPT. This helps you study important information and avoid spending time on useless subjects. It is critical to gather all the information you can and share it with your class.

• **High Threat** – The opposite of Low Threat – screwing something up so badly that you can get tossed out of the program or Air Force.

• **Intel** – Same a gouge.

• **Instrument crosscheck** – Process of logically, methodically checking the various cockpit display gauges that show current flight conditions during weather conditions. Critical to safe flight in bad weather.

• **Joe Bag of Doughnuts** – The average guy. "It is so simple, any Joe Bag of Doughnuts can do it."

• **Joint Specialized Undergraduate Pilot Training - JSUPT** - Pilot training program where Marine Corps and Navy student pilots attended Air Force training and visa versa.

• **Joker Fuel** – a prebriefed amount of fuel that, once reached, the current maneuver must be terminated and transitioned to the next phase of flight. For example, if you are doing aerobatics in the area, you will set an amount of fuel that when you reach it, you must return to the field for landings. That is joker fuel and you will set one for each phase of your flight.

- **Line** – A flying period during the day. "I'm flying on the first line".

- **Low Threat** – A task or event that has little danger of hurting your aviation career or overall success in UPT.

- **Manifestation of Anxiety** – MOA – A fear or negative physical reaction to the flying environment. It can be active (airsickness) or passive (being scared to fly).

- **Mission Hacker** – Person who puts out 100% effort everyday. Hard worker with a great attitude that gets the heavy lifting done. Definitely a good term that you want attached to your reputation.

- **Mission Qualified, mission qual, MQ** – Pilot status when you are qualified to fly your assigned aircraft as a weapon of war. Attaining this status is your main goal once you are assigned an aircraft.

- **NOTAMS – Notices to Airmen** – Information messages published for the aviation environment that informs pilots of changes or abnormal occurrences at airports, the aviation infrastructure, or navigation aids. Before conducting any flight a pilot must check the NOTAMS for the flight.

- **Nugget** – Your head, melon, brain bucket, etc.

- **OTS** – Officer Training School

- **Paper tiger** – A life-sized, paper mock-up of an aircraft's interior.

- **Pro Gear (Professional Gear)** – The individual, personal items a pilot uses during flight. Individual preference, different missions and aircraft can vary the equipment. Watches, sunglasses, and helmet bags all fall into this category.

211

- **Queep** – Trivial jobs, taskings, and requirements that, little by little pull the focus of your time and attention away from your primary mission, on to the trite and meaningless.

- **ROTC** - Reserve Officer Training Corps

- **Shit Hot, Sierra Hotel** – Pilot speak for outstanding, well-done, fantastic!

- **Situational Awareness** - SA - To understand the bigger picture of what is going on around you during a flight. This is a critical capability in complex, dynamic areas, such as flying. Your ability to keep your SA is major determining factor of your ability to fly.

- **Snacko** – Widely considered to be the lowest rung on the additional duty ladder. Officer charged with keeping the squadron snack bar stocked and the money generated accounted for.

- **Sortie** – An individual flight or aircraft movement. Interchangeable word with "flight".

- **Specialized Undergraduate Pilot Training** - **SUPT** - Name given to pilot training that splits training into the T-38 and T-1 training tracks after Phase II.

- **Speed Jeans** – Slang for G-suit.

- **Squeaker landing** – A very soft landing.

- **Sturon (or STUS)** – Verbal shorthand for the student squadron. You will be assigned to the student squadron while at flight school. The Sturon handles all your administrative support while in flight school and the start of your follow-on schools.

- **Track Night** – The event at the conclusion of Phase II in pilot training where students are informed of their track aircraft – T-38C (Fighter/Bomber) or T-1 (Tanker/Airlift).

• **TOLD, Take Off and Landing Data** – Calculated data that derives the distance required to take off and land on a given day. Some notable factors that go into this calculation; aircraft weight, runway length & slope, wet surface, pressure altitude, elevation and engine performance. This is a very critical and exact science.

• **Touch down landing zone** – The first 3000 feet of the runway, measured from the first load-bearing section of the runway. Any landing beyond 3000 feet is considered "long".

• **Undergraduate Pilot Training - UPT** – Flight School!

• **Unsat, Hook, Taco, Bust, Busted, Tube, Bone, Unsatisfactory**– any one of the 100 ways to say you failed at some aspect of training.

• **USAFA** - Air Force Academy

• **Wash back** – To be rolled into a later class. This can be for any number of reasons and should not be looked upon necessarily as a negative.

• **Wash Out** – Fail out of pilot training.

• **Zero Day** – Your first day of SUPT! What you have been working towards for many years!

READING AND MOVIES

- Fighter Pilot – Robin Olds

- Thud Ridge – Jack Broughton

- Going Downtown – Jack Broughton

- The Blue Max – Jack D. Hunter

- Stuka Pilot – Hans-Ulrich Rudel

- The First and the Last – Adolf Galland

- Yeager – Chuck Yeager

- Top Gun

- An Officer and a Gentleman (Just the altitude chamber part)

- Band of Brothers

- 300

- Fighter Pilot – IMAX

- YouTUBE – "Fighter Pilot"

- YouTUBE – Sh!t Fighter Pilots Don't Say

- YouTUBE - Sh!t IFS Students Don't Say

Made in the USA
Columbia, SC
28 March 2021

35196253R00128